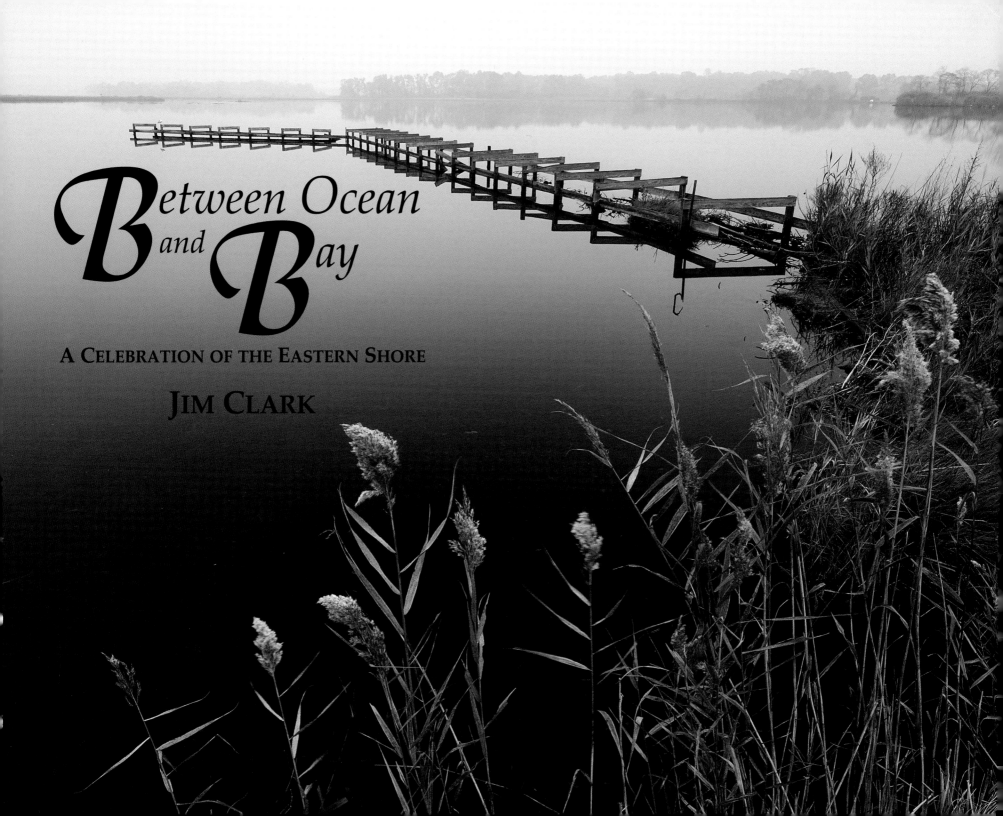

Between Ocean and Bay

A Celebration of the Eastern Shore

Jim Clark

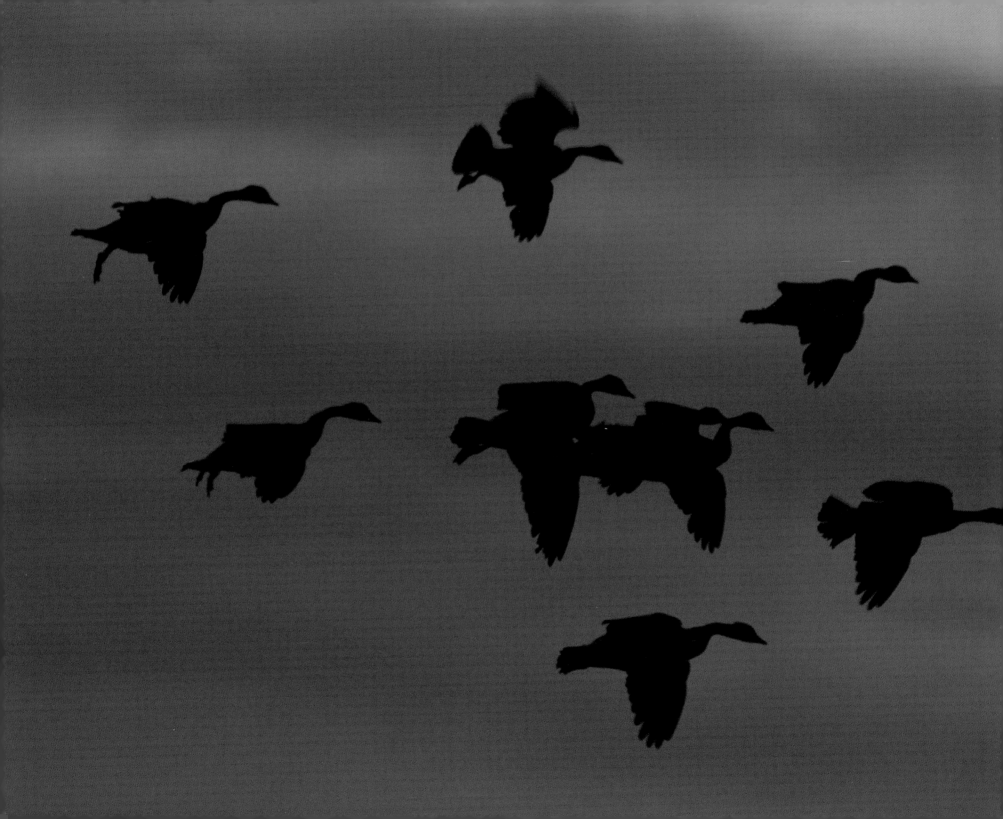

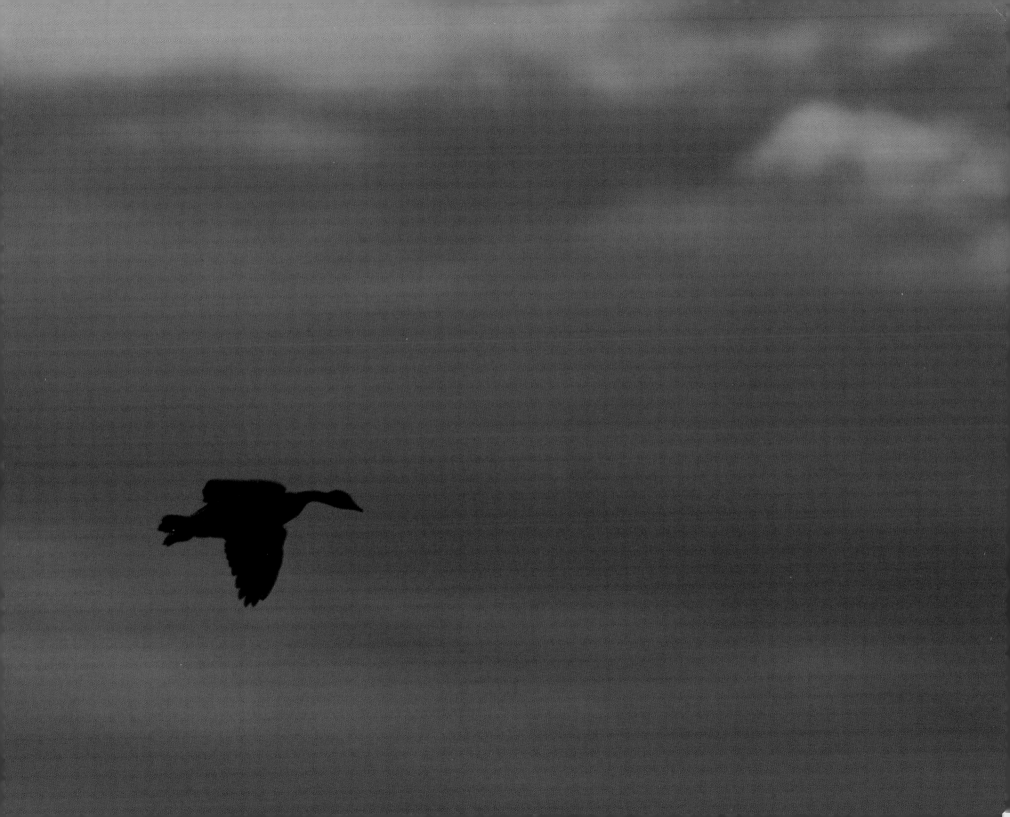

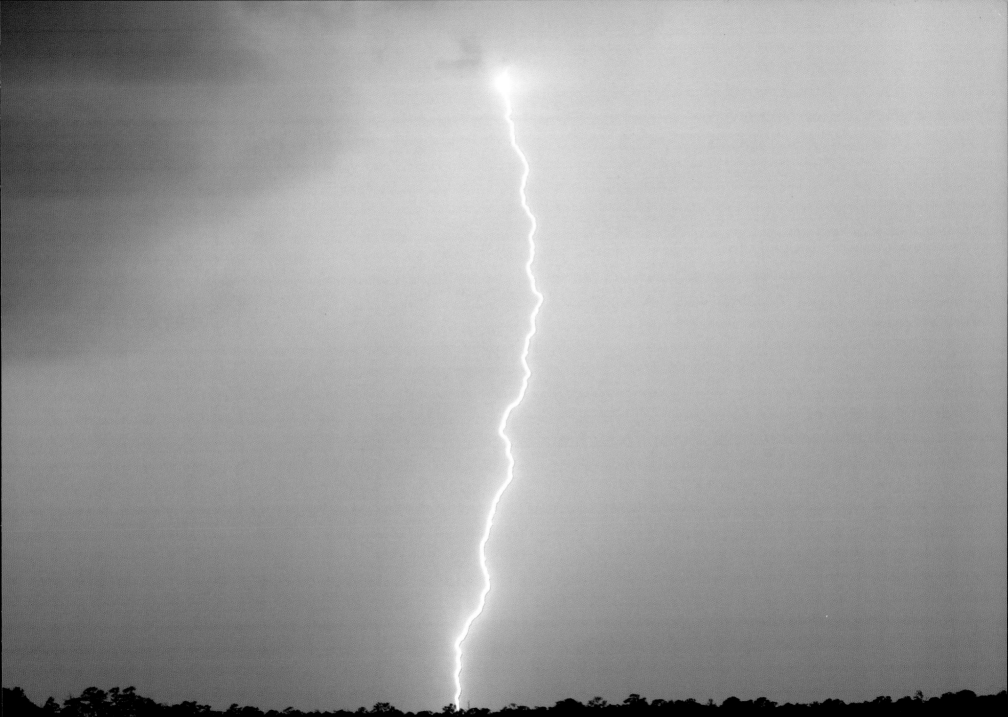

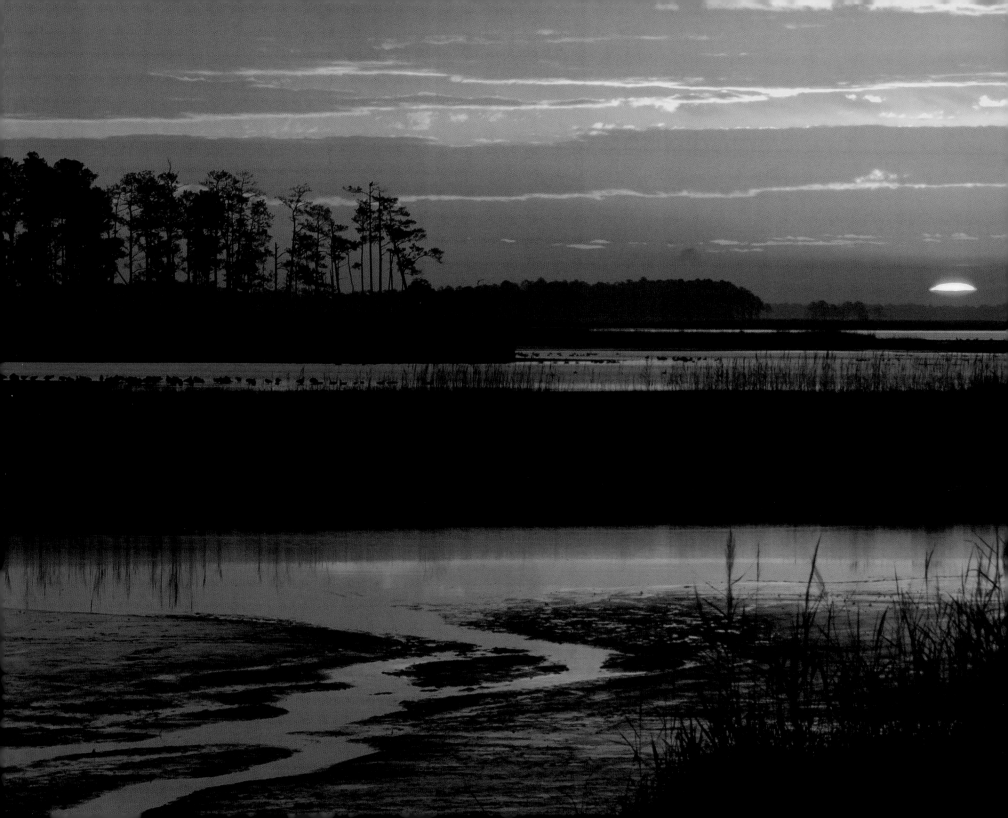

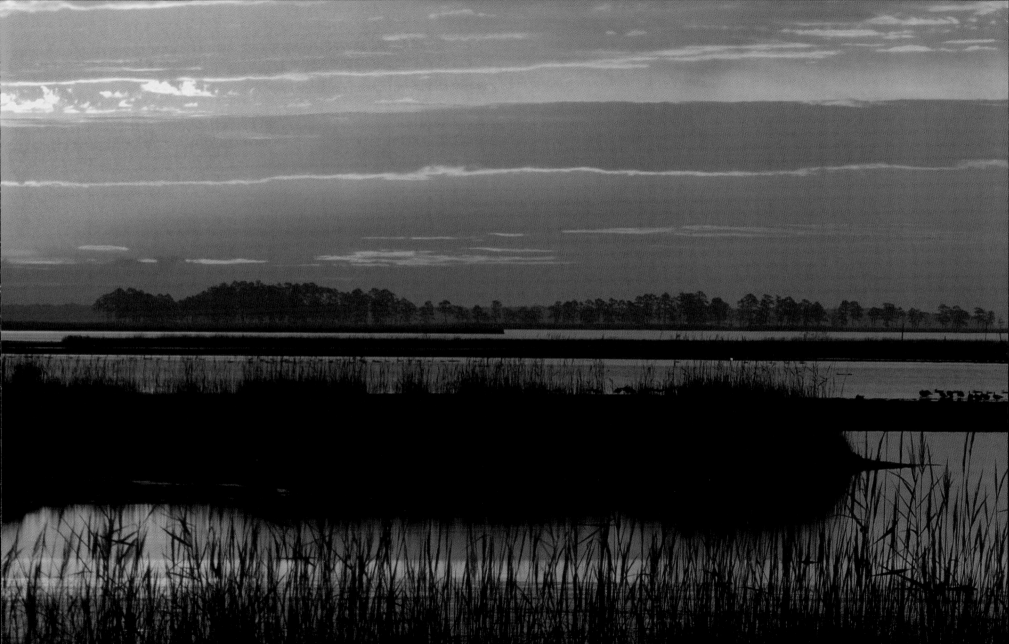

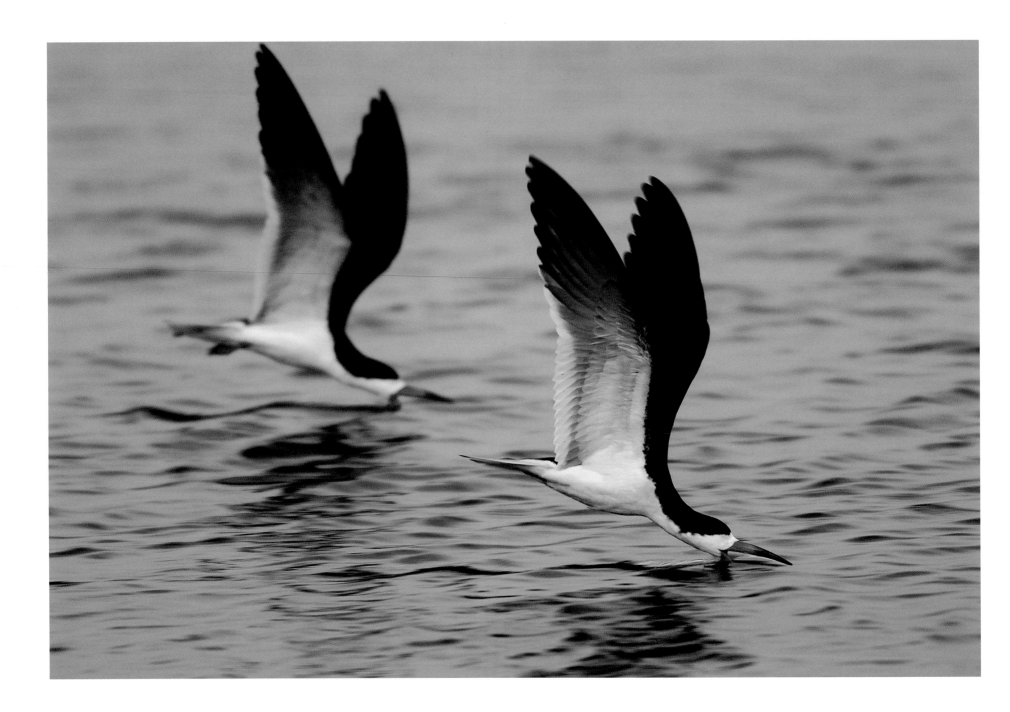

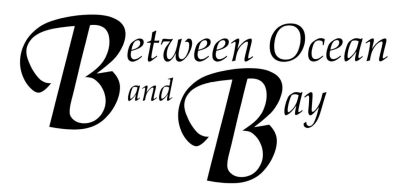

Between Ocean and Bay

A CELEBRATION OF THE EASTERN SHORE

JIM CLARK

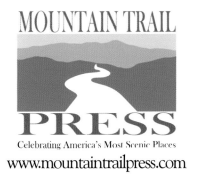

MOUNTAIN TRAIL

PRESS

Celebrating America's Most Scenic Places

www.mountaintrailpress.com

Book design: Ian J. Plant
Editor: Abbey Jones
Entire contents © 2008 Mountain Trail Press
Photographs and text © Jim Clark
All Rights Reserved
No part of this book may be reproduced in any form
without written permission from the publisher.
Published by Mountain Trail Press
1818 Presswood Road
Johnson City, TN 37604
ISBN: 978-0-9799171-5-8

Printed in Korea
First Printing, Fall 2008

Title Page: Foggy morning in Dorchester County, Maryland.
First frontispiece: Canada geese flying in formation at sunrise,
Blackwater National Wildlife Refuge, Maryland.
Second frontispiece: Lightning strikes over Blackwater Marsh.
Third frontispiece: Sunrise along the auto tour road,
Blackwater National Wildlife Refuge.
Left: A pair of black skimmers, Chincoteague National
Wildlife Refuge, Virginia.

*D*edication

To my fellow explorer and good buddy, my son Carson

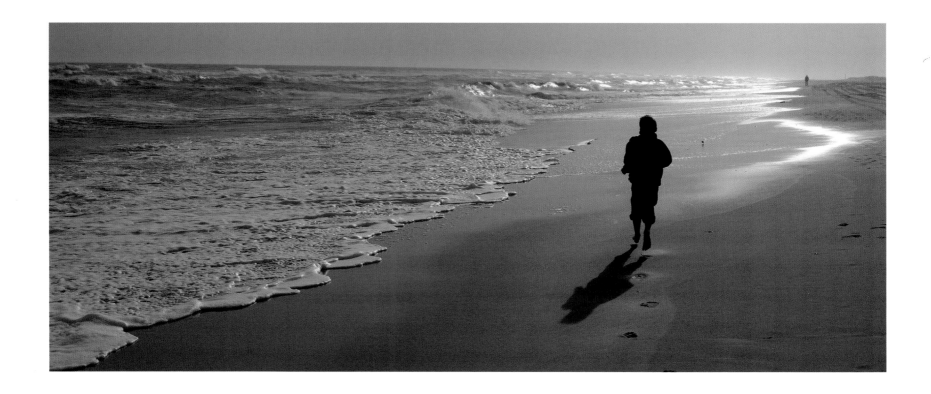

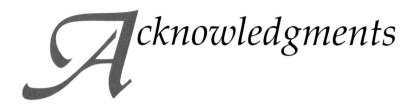cknowledgments

I want to highlight a few individuals who have enlightened my world and made me want to use my skills as a photographer and writer to inspire others. The one person these days that ignites the spark in my heart is my son, Carson. Thanks Carson for bringing out the child-like wonder in me. I am one lucky Dad to have a wonderful son such as you. You are my best buddy. I look forward to more father-son photo-treks around the country.

Without the support and encouragement of my beautiful wife, Jamie, I would still be years behind in making this book a reality. Thanks Jamie, for always standing beside me and telling me when it's time to take a break and when it's time to get back to work. The world owes you a big thanks for your lifetime of hard work to protect our global natural heritage. So, on behalf of the world, thank you.

My love goes to my mother, Pauline Clark, who for the past 93 years has brought joy and hope to everyone she has met around the world. You are one lucky person if you have ever met her. If you haven't, you are missing out on a wonderful experience. Thanks also to my adopted big sister, Polly Vance, who for years let me get away with all the mischievousness afforded a young boy growing up in the coalfields of West Virginia. My thanks and love goes to my sister Helen Hickman: still the best twin-sister in the world. Thanks go to my other siblings: brothers Norman & Charles, and Sister Joyce.

I would like to express my appreciation to Bishop James J. Shand of the Diocese of Easton and Reverend Bob Gribbon of Old Trinity for permission to include the image of the cemetery at the Old Trinity Church in Church Creek, Maryland.

I would like to thank my former staff at the National Conservation Training Center for their support, encouragement, and friendship: Jaime Brown, Liz Fritsch, Karen Lindsey, Judy Sager, and Steve Wunderley. Thanks for making my job much more enjoyable and rewarding.

I want to express my gratitude to the following folks for their friendship and support during the years I explored the Eastern Shore: Cork and Lola McGee of Chincoteague and their daughters Teresa and Amy; Chincoteague native Donna Leonard; the fine staff at the Refuge Inn in Chincoteague; current and former national wildlife refuge project leaders Glenn Carowan, John Schroer, Sue Rice, and Martin Kaehny; Sally Bowden of Chincoteague National Wildlife Refuge and Angela Graziano of the U.S. Fish and Wildlife Service's Washington Office; and our wonderful neighbors Eileen and Jack Gudat. I would like to thank Dr. Gaby Chavarria, one of the world's most renowned conservation biologists, who graciously helped me confirm identification of the insect species I observed and photographed on the Eastern Shore. Finally, thanks to composer Gary Malkin for his expressive music that eloquently graces the many programs I present across the country, including my program about the Eastern Shore. You are a kindred spirit.

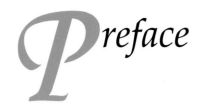 *reface*

Few regional names in America clearly define a significant sense of place and time in our national consciousness as does the Eastern Shore. But what makes it so? Is it the association with the Chesapeake Bay and the hundreds of impressive, almost incomprehensible, superlatives that frame our nation's largest, longest, most productive estuary? Or is it something else?

For me the region's character and people define the Eastern Shore's soul and spirit. Founded on more than 300 years of traditions, the people have been so consciously devoted to their way of life and to their rugged independence that the region's geographical isolation seems only to have been enhanced. But whether devoted or indifferent, the people are inextricably tied to the environment and inevitably influenced by their past, two traits extremely important to me. Simplicity of life has been retained, a mode of life unique and graceful, and standards of character and ethics that are still important today.

The fabled Eastern Shore is a beckoning region of abundant wildlife and lovely beaches, of farms and seaside communities, of waterman and farmers. While appealing to many, the landscape reveals itself slowly, if at all, to the outsider; a fact that for some inexplicable reason never seemed to be quite applicable to me. For years I wondered why that was so, especially since my upbringing in clannish eastern North Carolina had conditioned me to expect nothing more than respect at best, but never acceptance as a local native. I often thought it was my long term affection for the area's abundant wildlife, fueled by the romanticism of Mitchner's *Chesapeake* and my adolescent fantasy to be a famous Chesapeake Bay market hunter that drew me repeatedly to seek a position at Blackwater National Wildlife Refuge. So one day I was amazed to learn that the ties binding me to this place go much deeper than I could have ever before imagined: It was my ancestry, and not just the fact that the area represented the birth of my family in America like so many other Irish, but also that my seventeenth century relatives had actually owned property that is now part of Blackwater Refuge.

I have called the Eastern Shore home for the past 18 years of my 37 year career with the U.S. Fish and Wildlife Service's National Wildlife Refuge System. The Eastern Shore is the one place that shaped my character in life more than any other. This place is truly home for me. My dear colleague, good friend, and extraordinary photographer Jim Clark has captured the spirit and heart of this special landscape through his words and images. His ability to capture the key ingredients of a composition that creates a sense of place is remarkable. His keen eye and thoughtful prose provide the right combination that describes the creatures, places, and people that make the Eastern Shore and our National Wildlife Refuges high standards of character that flow into the current of our national life. I trust you will enjoy these scenes and stories as much as I.

Glenn Carowan
Project Leader – 1989-2007
Blackwater National Wildlife Refuge

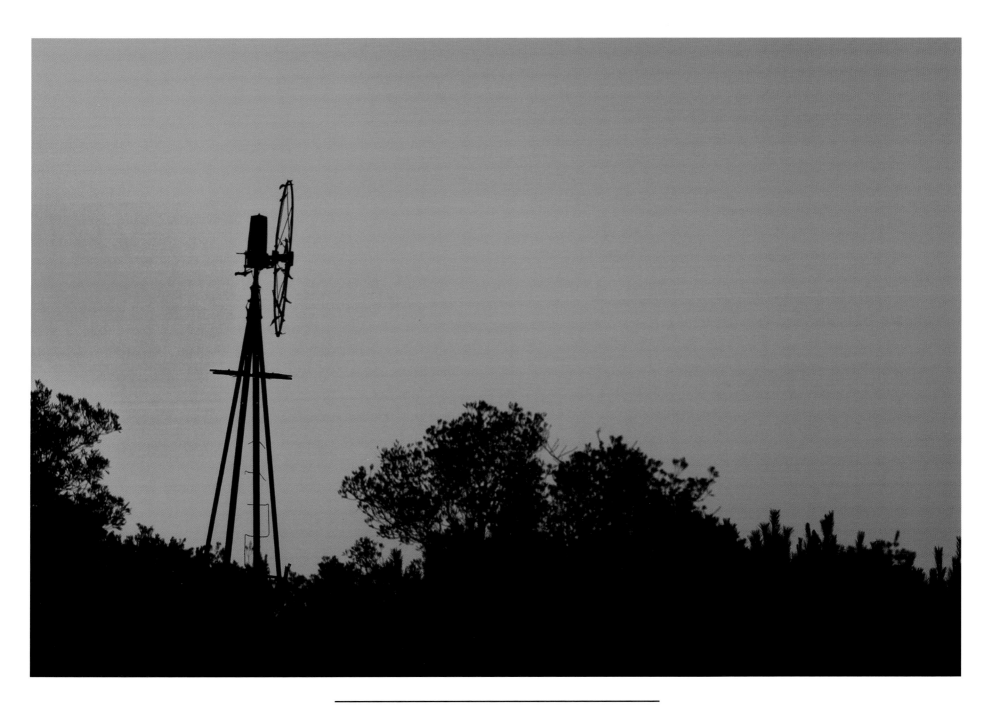

Windmill at sunrise, Chincoteague National Wildlife Refuge, Virginia.

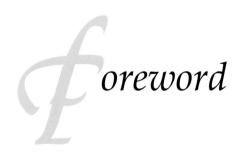

*F*oreword

I was first introduced to the magic of the Eastern Shore in 1976, when I was the Assistant Refuge Manager of the Back Bay National Wildlife Refuge in Virginia Beach. While this refuge is not officially located on the Eastern Shore, one of its satellite refuges, Fisherman's Island National Wildlife Refuge, was. My visits to this island sparked my love for this landscape. Although I left the region a few times in my 36-year career, I returned once again in 1988, serving as the Project Leader for the Chincoteague National Wildlife Refuge. I remained in that position for 16 years until my retirement.

The Eastern Shore is very unique. The Eastern Shore lies in close proximity to millions of people; however, this region is also strategically located along the Atlantic Flyway, thereby benefitting millions of migratory birds each year. The Eastern Shore is also blessed with many protected areas, including nine different National Wildlife Refuges. All told, the Eastern Shore provides opportunities for recreation, conservation, and solitude.

I first met Jim Clark many years ago. He, like me and many others, was totally dedicated and devoted to the National Wildlife Refuge System. He was also in charge of training the young people coming into the System. I admired the way in which Jim instilled in those young impressionable minds his love for and his dedication to national wildlife refuges. I also came to know Jim as a phenomenal nature photographer, one who had the patience to wait for the right moment rather than disturb the wildlife to "create" the shot. The images in this book are a true testament to his abilities with a camera.

What is that "something" that draws people back to the Shore? Well, Jim has truly captured that "something" in the images in this magnificent book. It's the beauty; it's the peacefulness and tranquility; it's the naturalness; it's the diversity of wildlife; it's the escape from the "real" world; it's all these and more. During the weeks and months that followed our Nation's tragedy on 9/11, people flocked to the Eastern Shore. I had the pleasure of talking to some of these folks, and their stories were the same. They needed to get away from the chaos of what this world had become and reconnect with the calming effects of nature. After hearing these stories, I began to stop and enjoy a sunset, or a great blue heron, or a flock of snow geese, or the ocean breeze a bit longer.

If you need a place to escape, consider a trip to the Eastern Shore or just pick up this book. Jim Clark's memories in both words and photographs have captured the essence of the area. As you leaf through this wonderful book, feel free to let your mind drift off to the marshes and woodlands and the diversity of wildlife that make the Eastern Shore so magnificent.

John Schroer
Project Leader – 1988-2004
Chincoteague National Wildlife Refuge

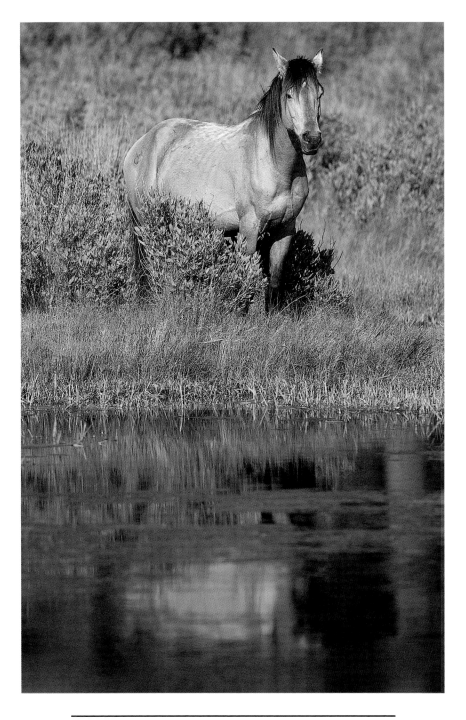

Wild horse, Chincoteague National Wildlife Refuge, Virginia.

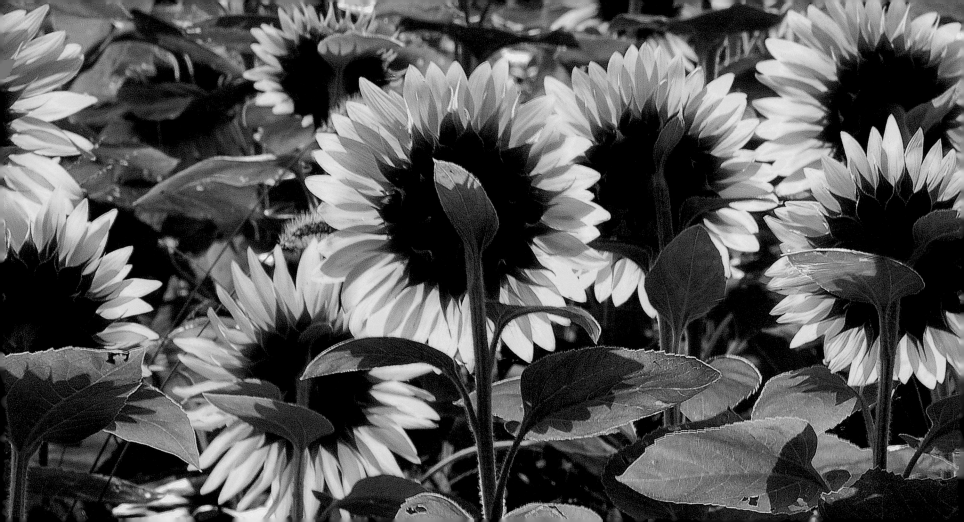

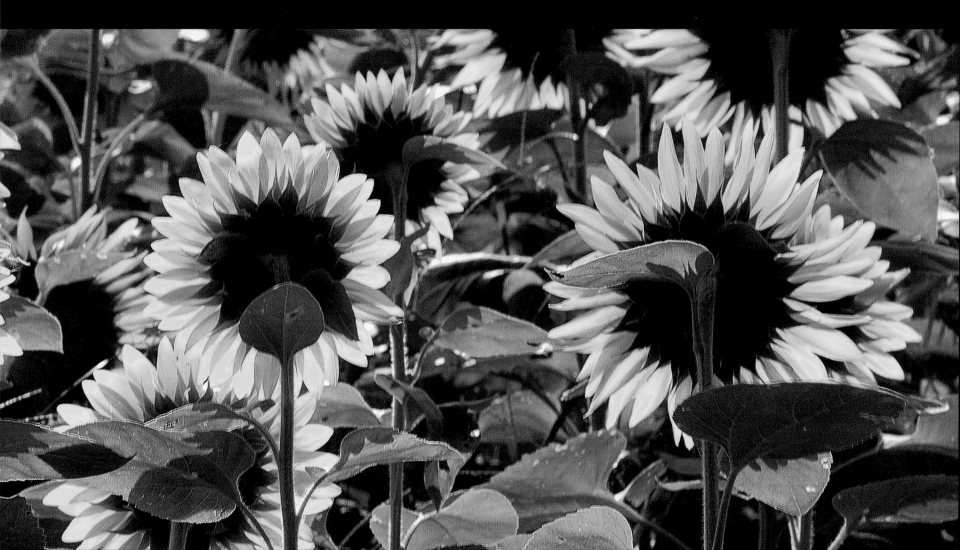

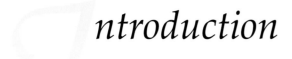ntroduction

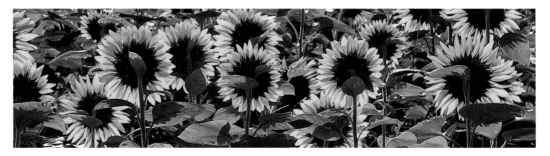

Along the backwaters of the Blackwater National Wildlife Refuge, a lone great blue heron silhouetted against the gray pre-dawn sky surveys the marsh below its perch, located high in a loblolly pine snag. While the heron remains silent and resolute, sounds of the marsh filter through the morning air, sweetening the moment with a harmonious collection of chirps, croaks, and whistles. As the somber skies yield to the rising sun, the heron shakes its feathers, stretches its wings, and lifts off from the pine bough. The morning, however, is not finished with its natural and pleasant distractions.

A bald eagle flies by as two more in the distance stand watch from a loblolly bough hanging over the marsh. Within seconds, another eagle soars over the marsh. The sun begins cresting above the horizon and while the season is autumn, songs of the marsh drift over the landscape: the sweet melodies and calls of song sparrows, mallards, brown-headed nuthatches, geese, flickers, and blue jays infuse the air. And lest I forget the red-winged blackbirds; what's a Chesapeake marsh without red-wings?

Later this same autumn morning, I find myself on the refuge's main road exploring hedgerows and odd areas for signs of activity to witness through my viewfinder. Along the edge of a cornfield near refuge headquarters, a light fog layer hovers just above ground level, maybe 12 feet in height at most. In the distance honking can be heard, and as the daylight slowly sears off the fog, flocks of Canada geese appear out of the thick veil of moisture, making their way to favorite feeding haunts outside the refuge. Along a hedgerow, a heavy coating of dew rests on the vegetation. Dew-covered grasshoppers cling to stalks of

goldenrod, mature way past their summer golden-drenched glory. The grasshoppers have a few more hours of inactivity until the sun is able to rise above the cool fog layer and warm the earth and their exoskeleton bodies.

In a small thicket of brambles, I discover a single green tree frog and praying mantis, both too chilled to move. Each appears to stand vigilant, not more than 6 inches separating insect from amphibian. They both make easy "prey" for a nature photographer (and each other), so I decide to help myself to this golden opportunity. I carefully position my tripod so as not to disturb them, but at the same time to provide me a nice composition of two dew-soaked critters. The two hours in this small patch of "weeds" prove enjoyable. Once again, the wonders of this fabled land have presented me with a unique opportunity to not only photograph, but to savor a natural celebration of life that is so pervasive here. But again, it is the Eastern Shore.

If only one word could be used to describe the Eastern Shore, *magic* would be the one I would select. This land between ocean and bay possesses a magical quality that is much more than its scenery; rather, it is a sum of all its parts – imposing coastal landscapes, natural diversity of wildlife, and seasons that bring personality to the land. As an individual who thrives on having mountains surrounding him, I discovered that the Eastern Shore breaks the mold; this landscape made me step outside my realm of comfort, gently prodding me to discover a world of golden marshes, fragrant piney woodlands, and quiet beaches. For more than 30 years I have enjoyed exploring its wild places, to savor its seasonal personality and to witness its natural wonders. Yes, there is relief in terms of topography here, but it's measured in units of tens of feet, not hundreds or thousands. But within its narrow spectrum of elevation lies a land of tremendous natural beauty and diversity.

The magnificence of the Eastern Shore, apparent to the perceptive eye, often remains shrouded to others for one reason: the landscape's lack of elevation. What may appear as a monotony of flatness, of seemingly expansive sameness with little relief, is actually anything but bland and featureless. For the undiscerning eye the landscape may be viewed as to possess nothing of interest, little to ignite the spirit or capture the imagination. But the landscape is deceiving unless you take time to explore it.

Flanked by the Chesapeake Bay on the west and the Atlantic Ocean on the east, the Eastern Shore formed through the combined forces of wind, water, and sand. These natural processes intertwined to establish the assortment of life now found in the Eastern Shore's salt marshes and shallow bays, forests, and sandy beaches. This splendid collection of life can sometimes seem well-concealed within the landscape's relatively simplistic exterior. But take a closer look and you'll discover this combination of subtle beauty and deceptive uniformity provides the ingredients to create an extraordinary family album of life.

The astonishing mix of wildness defining the character of the Eastern Shore occurs in both marine and freshwater marshes, on the beaches, along the edges of tidal flats, inside the forests of loblolly and oak, and within the weedy growth flourishing in abandoned fields and meadows. Wherever *terra firma* exists, a

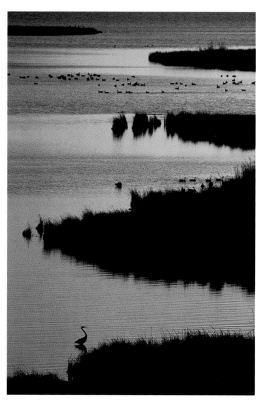

variety of wild creature will use it. Wherever the tides change, marine life abounds. Each time summer turns to fall and winter to spring, the skies above the Eastern Shore provide pathways for millions of migrating birds. The wild character and characters of the Eastern Shore offer up something each day of the year.

The seasonal gathering of wildlife on the Eastern Shore – especially birds – has few equals on the North American continent. During the autumn and spring seasons, bird migration is eagerly anticipated by both Shore residents and visitors. Songbirds, shorebirds, wading birds, and waterfowl seek the Eastern Shore's habitats for sustenance, rest, and reproduction. The shore's prominent location along the eastern seaboard creates a most favorable travel route for these determined and resolute travelers. Because of this, the Eastern Shore is also a favorite destination for birders to let loose their heart-felt passion. The Eastern Shore is always mentioned in the same breath as other world renowned birding areas.

The shore's combination of marsh, field, beach, and forest offers up a tempting arrangement of habitats that migratory birds find much to their liking. There's a little of something for each species. Marshes and bays provide respite for hundreds of thousands of ducks, geese, and swans. All wetlands entertain hordes of wading birds, from great blue herons to glossy ibis to green herons. Tidal flats and beaches offer welcome relief for millions of shorebirds migrating, and the beaches provide critical habitat for rare nesting shorebirds such as piping plovers. The shore's maritime forests create the right substrate for countless

Sunset at Blackwater National Wildlife Refuge, Maryland.

migrating and nesting songbirds. During the evening hours of spring and summer, chuck-will-widow's and great horned owls call out from the loblolly and hardwood forests. Birdlife abounds here 24/7.

Other winged migrants also track the topography of the Eastern Shore to their favorite wintering retreats further south. The narrowing peninsula forming the Eastern Shore becomes a virtual roadmap for millions of migrating monarch butterflies. Fluttering down the Eastern Shore, these graceful flying rays of sunshine collect in mass at the tip of the peninsula before making a final push across the Chesapeake Bay to reach their wintering home in Mexico. This most ancient and mysterious natural event continues to amaze us landlocked creatures. Regardless of the season, however, the Eastern Shore is a wildlife watcher's dream with a long list of state, federal, and privately protected lands set aside for wildlife. With an ever-increasing human population and the subsequent development of housing and shopping malls, these protected places become even more important, and in some cases, threatened.

Throughout the length of the Eastern Shore are national wildlife refuges, state parks, and the Assateague Island National Seashore – each managing and protecting important wildlife habitats. These places literally serve as wildlife oases in an ever increasing sea of humanity. With names such as Blackwater, Chincoteague, Eastern Neck, and Eastern Shore of Virginia, national wildlife refuges and other protected lands carry out conservation programs to ensure the shore's natural inhabitants, both resident and migrant, have what they need to survive. And these places are not just for wildlife, either.

Like many of our national treasures throughout the country, the Eastern Shore also offers its human visitors a chance for solitude and personal discovery. Most importantly, these havens offer a chance to nurture awareness and foster concern for these and

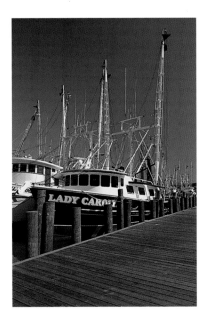

other important and fragile ecosystems. These places encourage investigation and exploration, and with each visit, you become reacquainted with the familiar and upon leaving, you will have learned something new. For the millions of visitors, the Eastern Shore's gracious and less frenetic pace, combined with the region's history, scenery, wildlife, tradition, and simplicity provide an outlet from a fast-paced world. As Captain John Smith wrote in 1608 about the Eastern Shore, *"Heav'n and earth never agreed better to frame a place for man's habitation..."*

For more than 30 years I have explored the Eastern Shore with not only binoculars, field guides, and notebook, but with a camera, expending roll after roll of film – and now flash card – capturing compositions of the region's special places. For the past 15 years I have led photography workshops here, bringing awareness to others around the country about this wonderful enclave of nature. Now, I want to share some of my experiences and imagery with you as well.

A journey through the wild places of the Eastern Shore requires visitors to use all their senses to savor the experience: to smell the fresh aroma of sandy soils and loblolly pine; to feel the softness of a fresh bed of fallen pine needles; to taste the salty air along a wind-swept beach; to listen to the symphony of life-songs from the region's extraordinary bird world; and to watch the amazing progression of wildlife that call the Eastern Shore home.

Join me now on a visual journey of discovery about this exceptional land called the Eastern Shore. Learn a thing or two about its wild inhabitants and landscapes. Add a tip here and there about photographing its wonderful cavalcade of life. But most importantly, revel in the joy that the Eastern Shore's wildlife, wildlands, seasons, and people offer up its visitors and residents alike. Once you visit the Eastern Shore, you'll return. And when you have to leave, you'll make an excuse to stay.

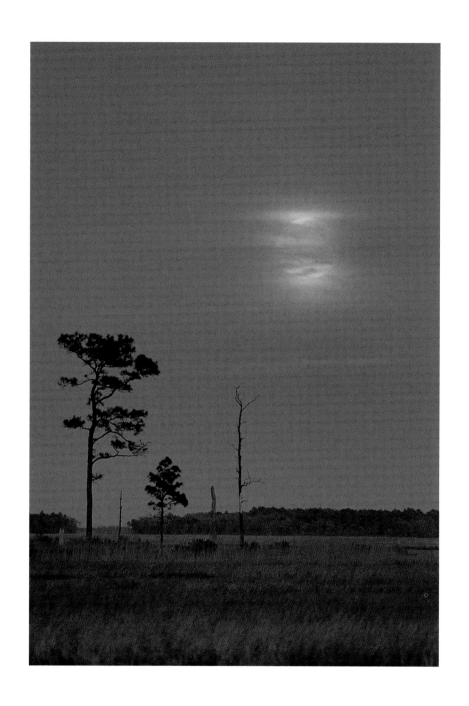

Left: Scallop boats, Chincoteague, Virginia.
Above: Spring moonrise, Blackwater National Wildlife Refuge, Maryland.

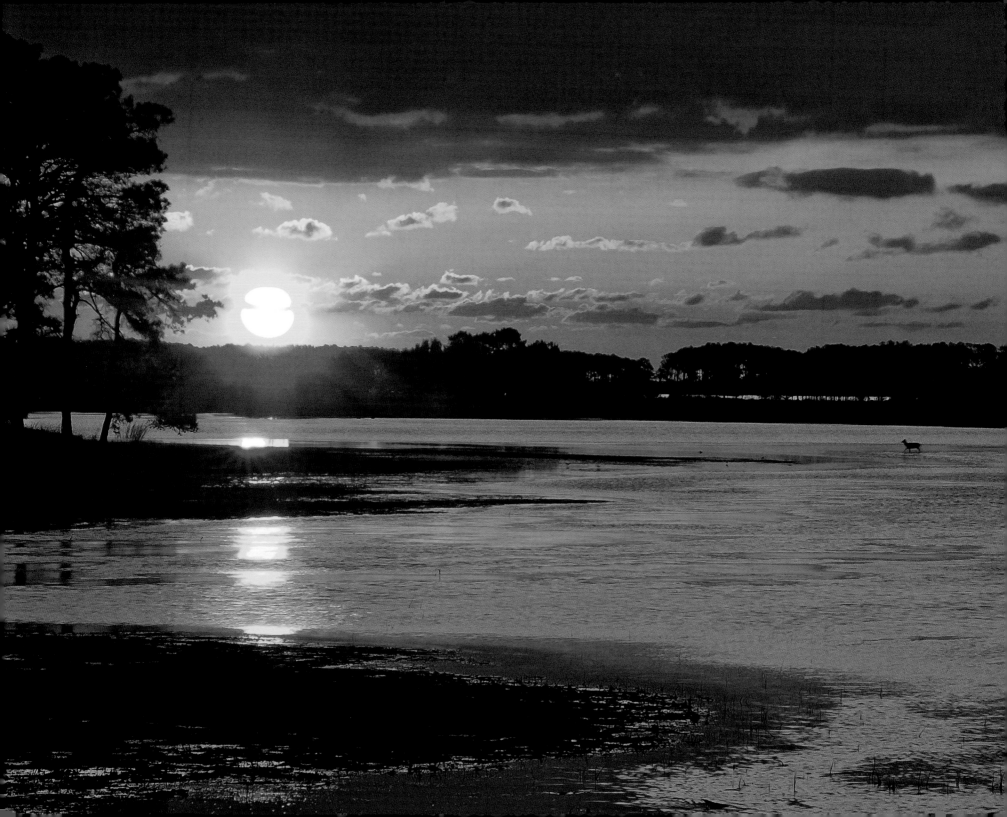

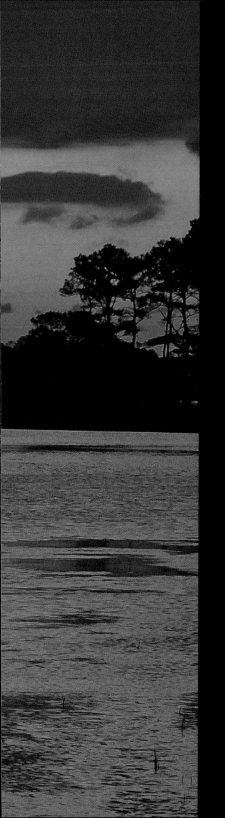
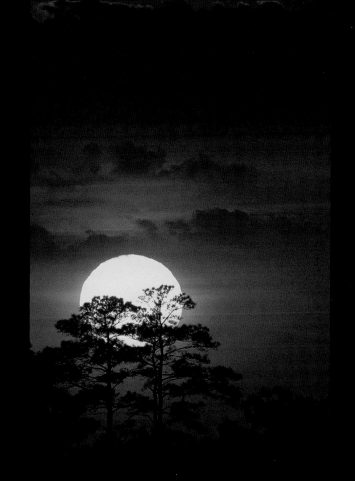

One of the most memorable experiences while visiting Chincoteague National Wildlife Refuge and Assateague Island National Seashore is to get up before dawn and drive to the beach to watch the sun rise over the Atlantic Ocean. An even more inspirational location is along Beach Drive Road near Black Duck Pool on the refuge. Here, the mixture of forest, marsh, salmon-colored skies, and scattered clouds can create an even more unforgettable sunrise. This is one location I always take my photography workshop participants to see.

The scene at Black Duck Pool includes two "hammocks" of loblolly pine woodlands, which add a nice compositional element to the scene. More times than not one or more Sika deer will stroll across the wetland while flocks of Canada Geese, mallards, and other waterfowl rest on the water's surface. Above the scene will be a variety of egrets or terns flying.

This particular scene represents all the major habitat types that are protected within the refuge. Because of this diversity of woodlands, marsh, and beach, the refuge is rich in numbers and types of wildlife species, especially birds.

Above: The day ends with the setting sun over distant loblolly pines.

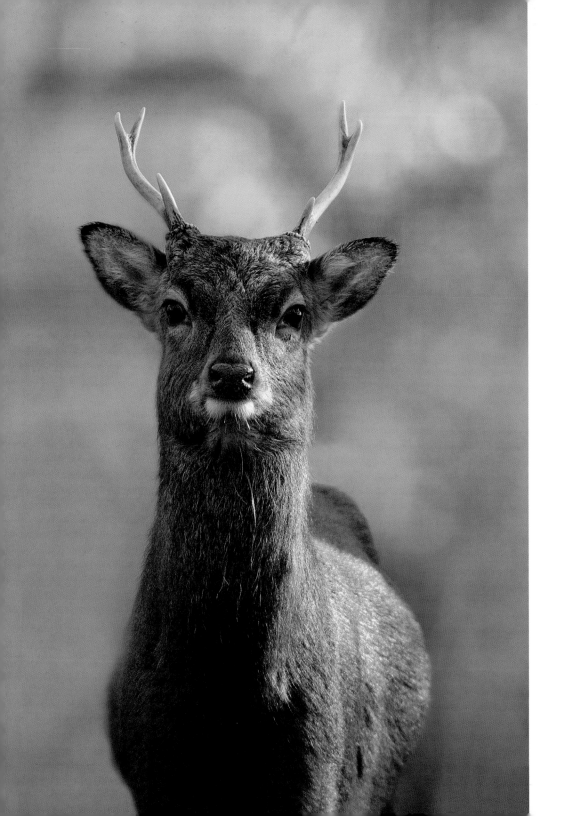

Sika deer were first introduced to the Eastern Shore in 1916 on James Island. Since that time, the sika deer has expanded its range throughout the Eastern Shore region. This Asiatic elk species prefers the marshlands and wet woodland habitats, while the native white-tailed deer, which is much bigger, prefers the drier woodlands and edges.

While spending an autumn morning hiking along the Woodland Trail at Chincoteague National Wildlife Refuge, I saw this spiked sika bull on a small sand hummock in the loblolly pine forest. For several minutes, I just photographed the critter at a distance. Not sure what to do, the bull kept watching me, not moving a muscle for several minutes.

I slowly started making my way to the bull and again, it never flinched an inch. With a 200-400mm telephoto zoom lens, I was able to capture some very nice compositions of the deer in its habitat as well as some nice portrait shots.

Eventually, the bull had enough of my intrusion and started snorting at me. At one point, the bull jumped straight up into the air, all four legs totally above ground. This is one behavior I had never witnessed in this species. The bull finally took several hops back into the recesses of the forest, before turning around to see what I was doing. By that time, I had shot more than 100 images of the bull and decided we would both call it a day.

The Delmarva fox squirrel once ranged from southeastern Pennsylvania south along the Delmarva Peninsula – the mid-Atlantic coastal region that comprises the state of Delaware and the eastern coastal reaches of Maryland and Virginia. The loss of woodland habitat critical to its survival caused the population to decline so rapidly that in 1967, it was declared an endangered species. By the late 1960s, the population had dwindled to less than thirty.

Today this beautiful silver-gray squirrel clings to existence in only four counties along Maryland's Eastern Shore (including Blackwater National Wildlife Refuge) and in Chincoteague National Wildlife Refuge in Virginia. Intensive restoration and management of coastal hardwood forests at both Blackwater and Chincoteague are helping to stem the decline of this gorgeous animal. Placement of nest boxes in the maritime forests also helps provide safe nesting sites for the squirrel.

Chincoteague National Wildlife Refuge offers the best opportunity to see the Delmarva fox squirrel. Hiking along the refuge's Woodland Trail will usually provide the hiker a glimpse or two of the squirrel as it scampers along the forest floor or scurries up a loblolly pine tree.

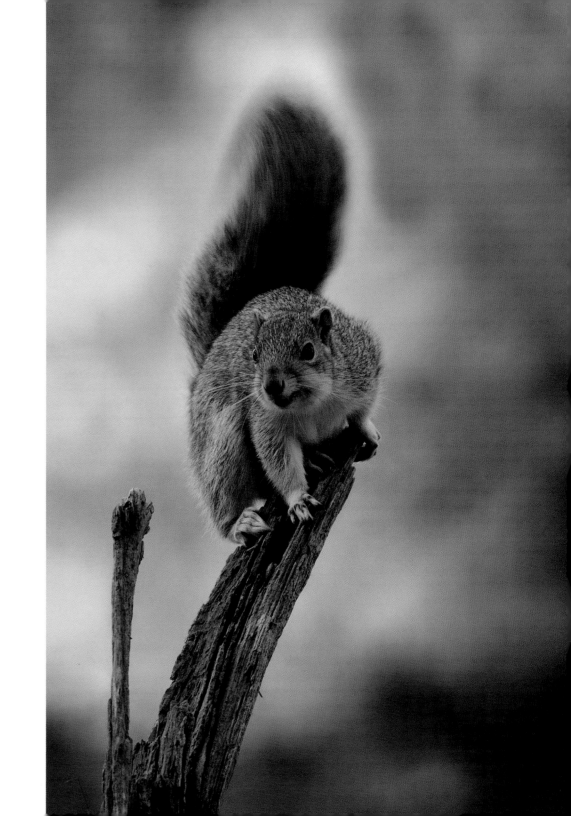

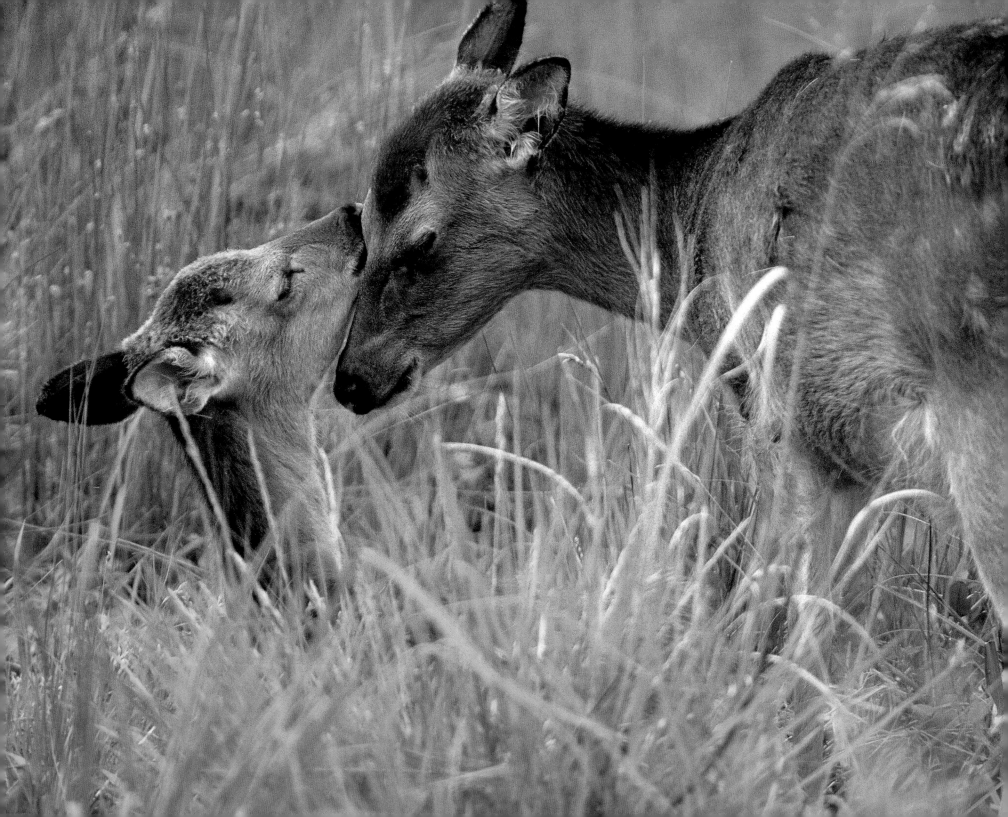

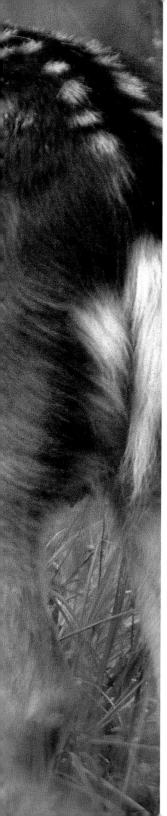

This image of a sika deer doe nuzzling its fawn is an example of how powerful nature images can help to lift the human spirit. On a cloudy spring day, while hiking along the auto-tour loop at Chincoteague National Wildlife Refuge, I saw this sika deer doe with its fawn resting in the tall grasses. A small group of hikers had also gathered along the edge of the road to watch the deer. I was lugging around my 600mm lens on a hefty tripod, so I welcomed the chance to take a break and to photograph the doe and fawn.

The deer weren't very active, so the hikers decided to continue on their journey around the tour route. I stayed a bit longer and within a few minutes, the doe stood up and started nudging the fawn. Suddenly, the fawn raised its head and started rubbing muzzles with its mother. I knew I had captured a wonderful moment in nature.

Months later, after I had given a presentation to a group, a lady from the audience approached me and mentioned how much she enjoyed seeing this photograph, which I included in the program. She asked if she could purchase the print and of course, I was happy to oblige. I was curious as to what attracted her to this image and she told me it reminded her of her love for her daughter, who was now recovering from a long and painful bout with cancer. She also mentioned that her daughter loved anything to do with deer, so the mother wanted this picture to present to her.

I was so struck by this story that I donated a large print to her and personally delivered it to her home. Ever since that day, I decided to always strive to use my images to inspire others to enjoy life as much as they can. No one is promised tomorrow, so make the most of every day.

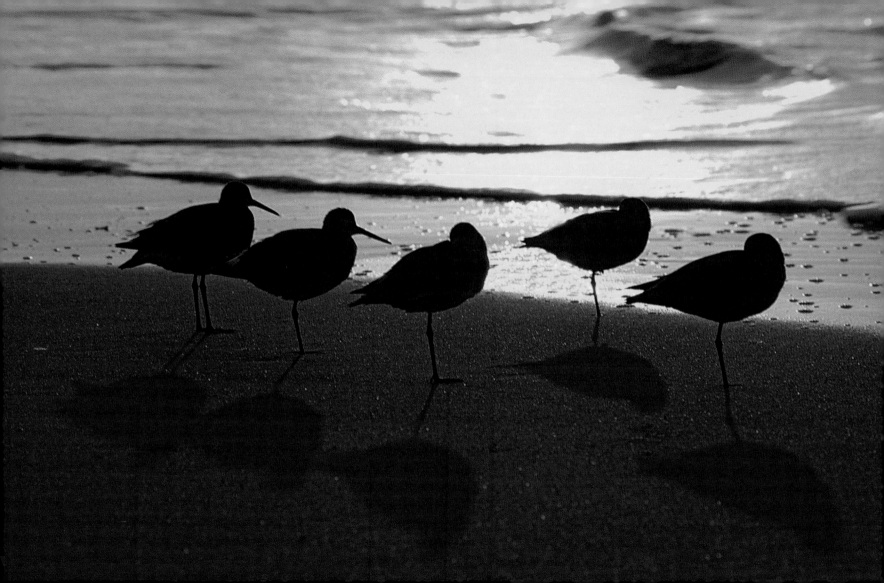

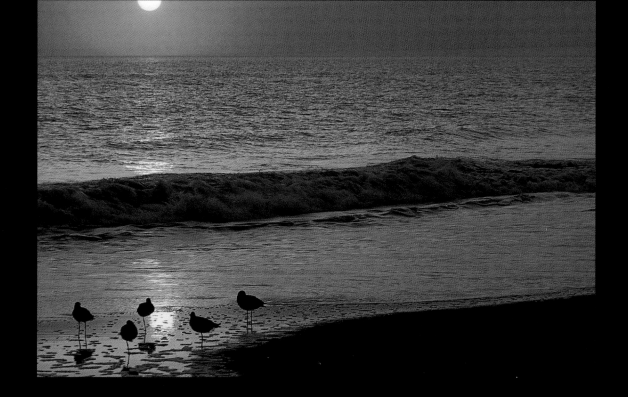

The willet is one of the most common shorebirds found along the Mid-Atlantic Coast. Although not very colorful, the willet is certainly entertaining, very noisy, and an important character among the lively cast of wild creatures of the region's marshes and beaches.

This particular group of willets was resting just beyond the reach of an early spring morning tide. Beyond the horizon, the sun began to paint a gold hue to the ocean and surrounding landscape. I had been photographing the scene with a wide-angle lens, but I decided to try my luck at composing an image highlighting the willets. With strong backlighting, I hoped to get a rather powerful composition of the willets in silhouette.

Getting on my knees, I slowly inched toward the birds. Forgoing a tripod, I decided to use my 80-400mm Vibration Reduction lens, hoping this new technology would perform up to its reputation to ensure sharp images at slow shutter speeds. It did.

The willets never seemed too distracted by me, but there was always one bird watching me. With the help of some very good knee pads, I spent about thirty minutes – still on my knees – photographing this wonderful group of shorebirds.

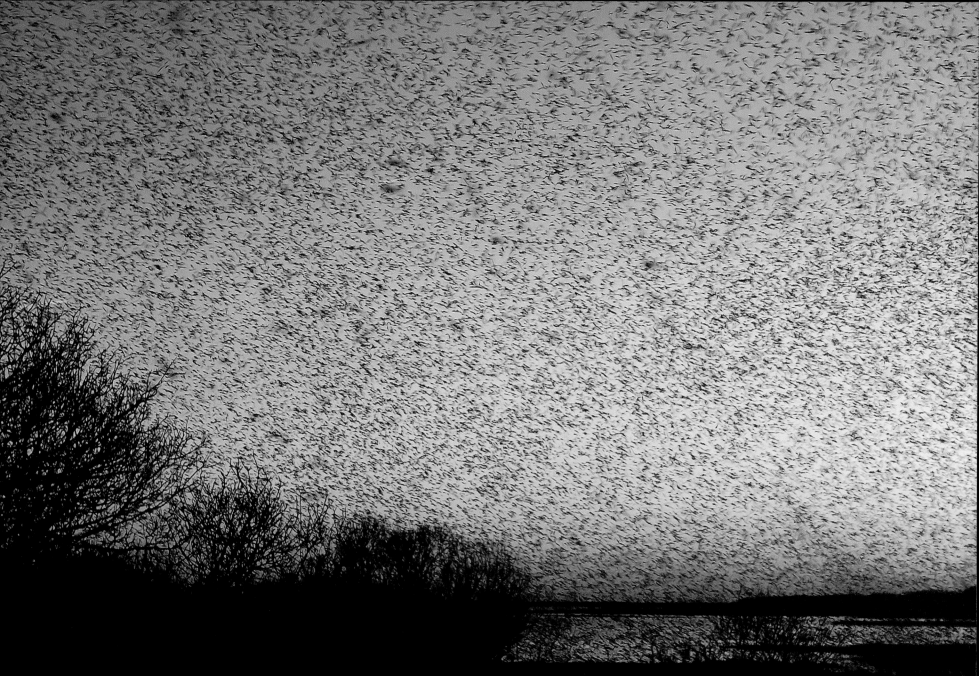

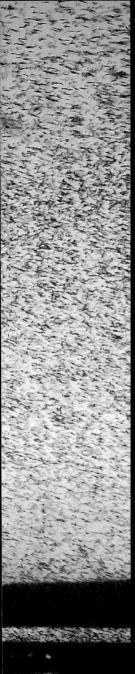

Anyone who spends time in the salt marshes of the Eastern Shore understands mosquitoes are part of the deal. From spring to late autumn, these blood-sucking insects can be expected to attack any exposed arm, leg, and face. While windy days, cool temperatures, and the winter months are usually the only times that a visitor can expect not to be assaulted, mosquitoes can be active anytime of the year. It's best to be prepared by having a long sleeve shirt, pants, and repellent nearby.

As annoying as they are, mosquitoes provide an important food source for the hundreds of bird species and other wildlife that occur here. The larvae are consumed by dragonflies, frogs, waterfowl, and shorebirds, while tree swallows and other avian aerial acrobats comb the air space above the wetlands for the flying adults.

One April afternoon, just as the sun was beginning to dip below the horizon, my friend and fellow photographer Marc Epstein and I were driving on Beach Road at Chincoteague National Wildlife Refuge. Along the portion of the road bisecting Swan Cove and Little Toms Cove, we saw what appeared to be several columns of black smoke rising above the edge of the road. We soon discovered that these were hatches of male mosquitoes. Knowing that the male mosquito is a nectar-feeder, we walked into a swarm and started photographing them. We got some very weird and

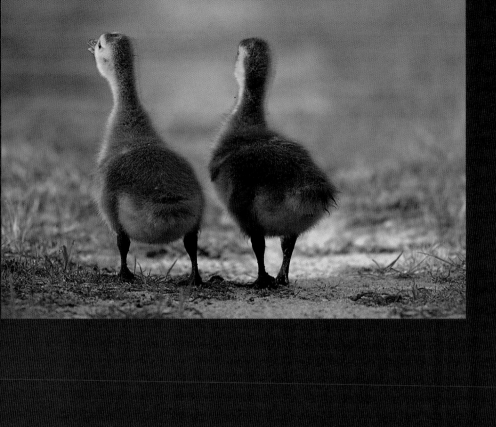

At one time autumn skies over the Eastern Shore were filled with thousands of migrating Canada Geese. The Canada's were heralded as a rite of passage, a change of seasons – the long strings of v-shaped formations signified that soon, winter would seize the land. The region's vast acreage of cornfields combined with the large tracts of protected wetlands provided the right mix of habitat for these long-distance travelers.

By the 1960s more than 100,000 migratory Canada geese wintered at the Blackwater National Wildlife Refuge alone. Aerial surveys since 1990 have shown a drastic decline in Canada geese – less than 26,000 now winter on the refuge. The issue these days throughout the Eastern Shore is the burgeoning population of non-migratory Canada Geese. Wildlife professionals, including myself, made the mistake of establishing non-migratory flocks of geese in areas where they normally did not reside year-round. The birds adapted to these new digs and eventually started reproducing at an alarming rate.

Before long, geese were found in residential parks, golf courses, and anywhere else that provided grass to graze and water to rest. A stroll through a park or a round of golf suddenly became a challenge in not getting goose droppings on one's shoes – or to be chased by a protective goose or gander.

Still, the sight of young gosling exploring their new world is something that brings joy to others. These two goslings were competing with each other while their siblings were busy grazing along the beach road at Chincoteague National Wildlife Refuge. The key to great wildlife photography is to sometimes get on the ground and photograph from the perspective of the animal, which is what I did to capture this moment of nature.

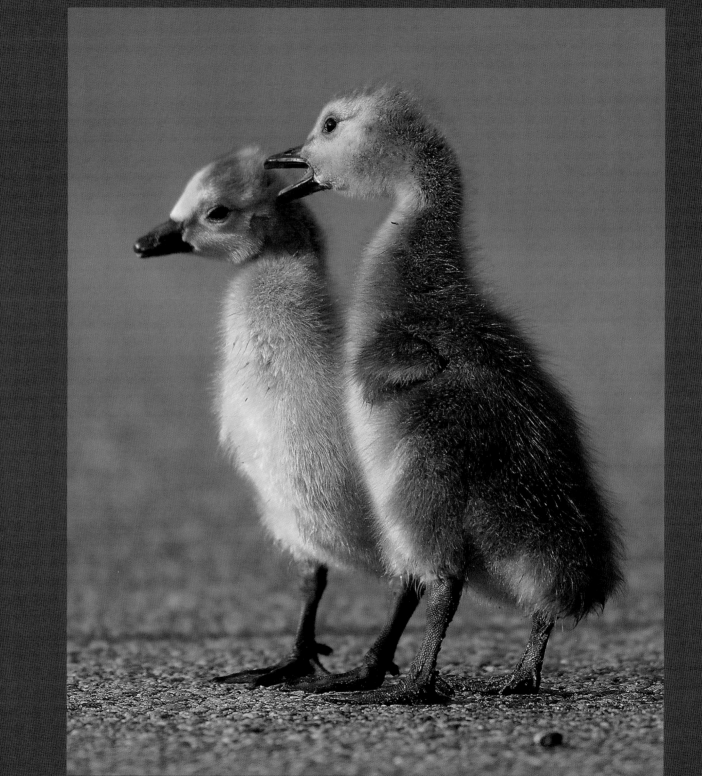

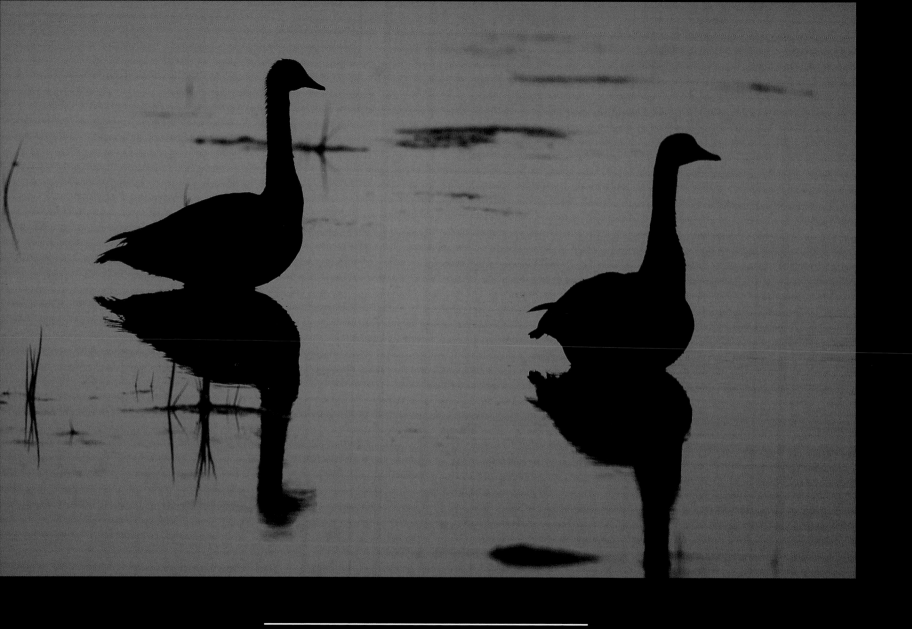

Canada geese at sunrise, Chincoteague National Wildlife Refuge, Virginia.

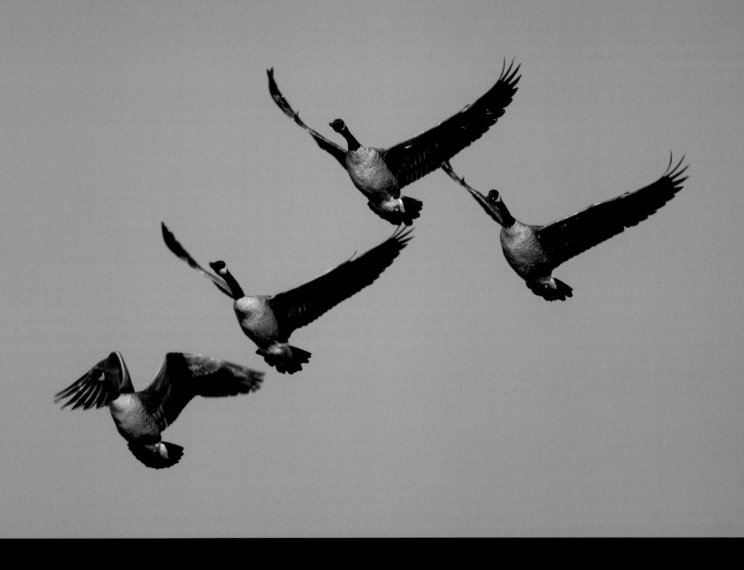

Canada geese in flight, Blackwater National Wildlife Refuge, Maryland.

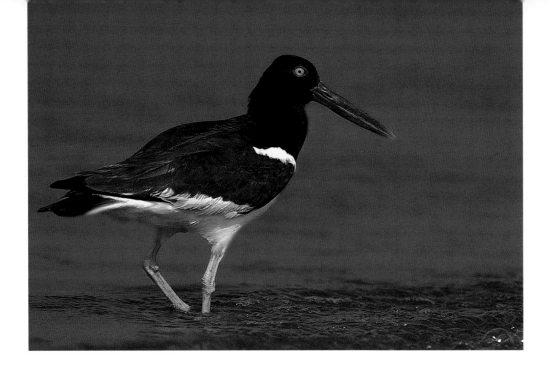

One of the most challenging birds to photograph is the belted kingfisher, a colorful critter that doesn't have much patience with humans intruding upon their space. But as I always emphasize to my workshop students, know when to chase a moment and when to anticipate one.

Both male and female kingfishers (the female has a brown chest band, whereas the male only has the blue band) were frequenting the channels bordering Beach Road on Chincoteague National Wildlife Refuge. While the winged anglers were okay with vehicles parked near their fishing perches along the channel, if anyone attempted to leave their vehicle and photograph them, the birds would take off and fly to another perch down the channel.

One day I discovered the male perched on one of his favorite fishing perches. I slowly raised myself beyond my vehicle's sunroof and captured some nice images, but it was the colorful female that I wanted. Throughout the week, I never got a chance to photograph her until the last hour of the last day I was there. While driving from the beach back to the hotel, I saw her sitting on a post in the channel. I carefully parked my vehicle off the road and placed my 600mm telephoto lens out the window. Using a 1.4 tele-converter to give me a bit more reach, I was able to take several photographs of her. The light was perfect and although she was still a considerable distance away, with the magic of digital photography I was able to crop a tight composition of her.

Above: American oystercatcher, Assateague Island National Seashore, Virginia.

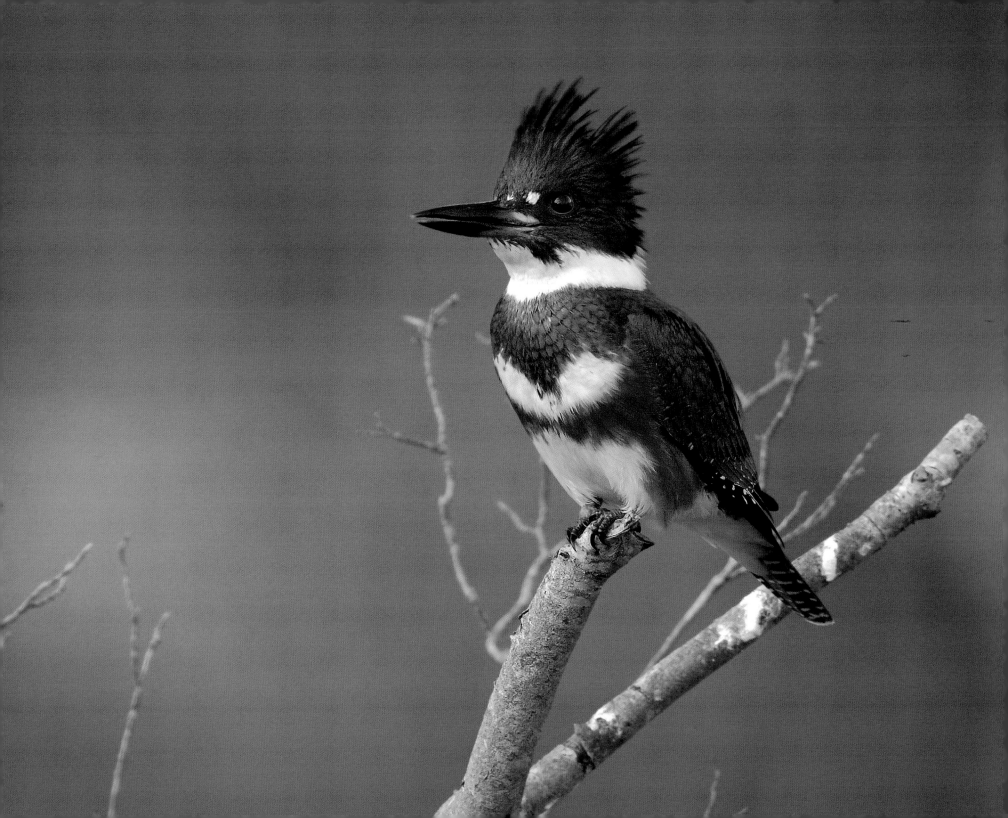

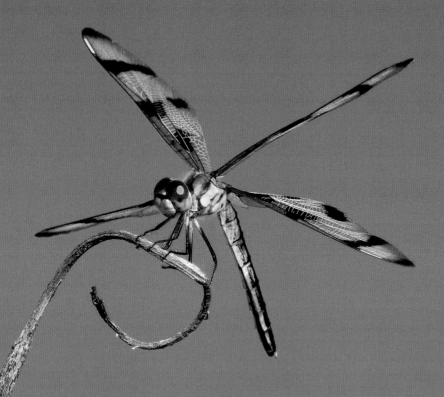

While most dragonflies and damselflies frequent open water, the eastern fork-tailed rarely does, preferring to stay near the wetland edges. Also, unlike other species of damselflies, the female eastern fork-tailed is rather common along wetlands. These slender blue-tipped insects are easy to miss since they are only a little over an inch in length and prefer to perch horizontally low on the vegetation.

During one late autumn afternoon, my friend Marc Epstein and I were photographing a river otter feeding in a wetland along the refuge's auto tour route. The otter suddenly slipped into a thicket of shrubs on the other side of the wetland. Not to be deterred, we decided to hang around for a while just in case the otter decided to re-enter the water.

As we waited for the otter to finish its dinner, I noticed several damselflies perched on the vegetation near my tripod legs. Carefully replacing my telephoto lens with a 200mm macro lens, I spent more than 30 minutes photographing these dainty insects, each barely longer than one inch. The green vegetation provided an excellent background for the composition. Eventually the otter slipped back into the water and Marc and I refocused our efforts from insects to mammals.

Above: Halloween pennant dragonfly.

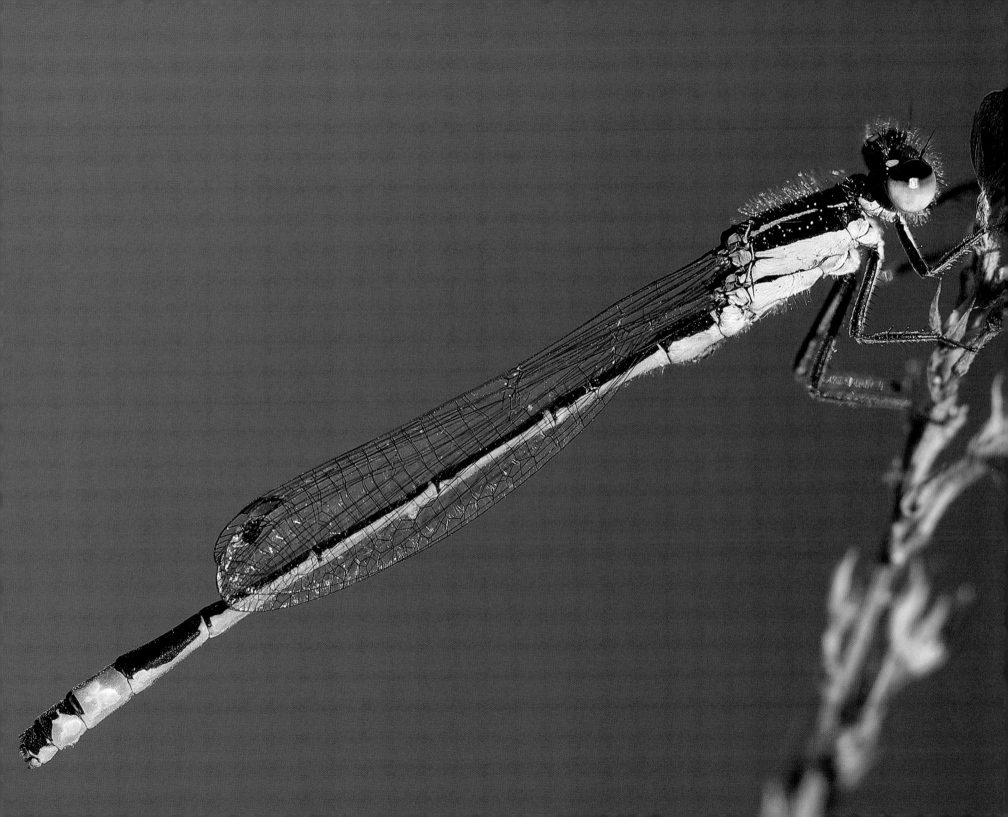

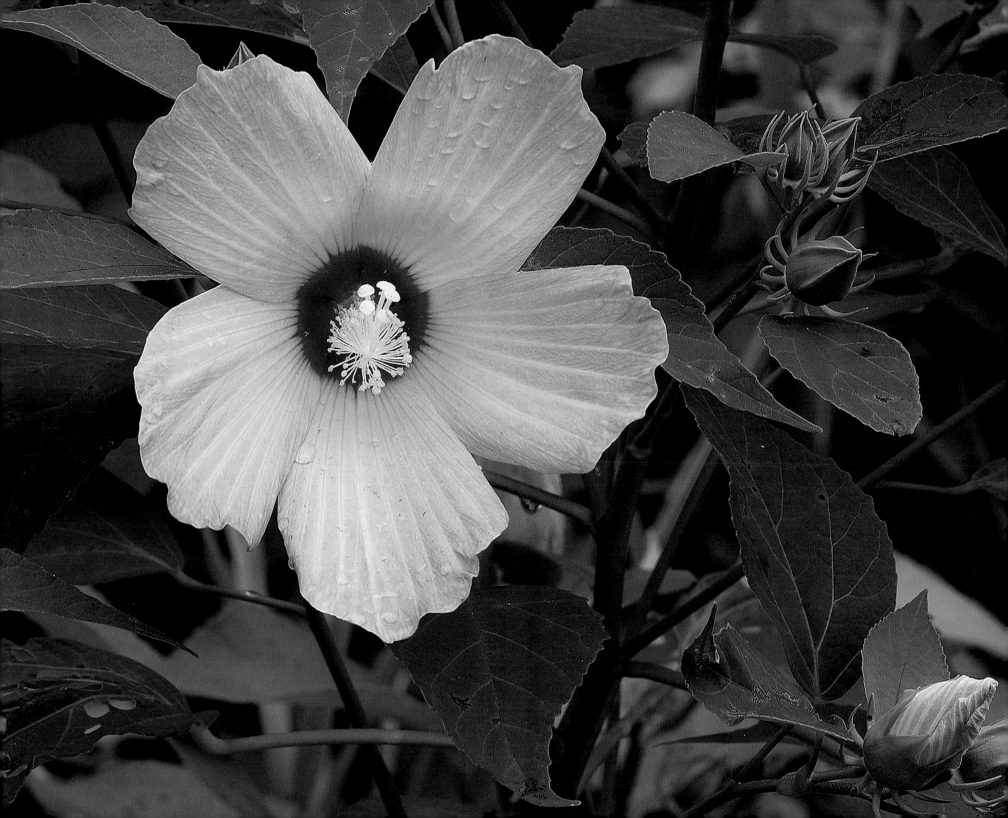

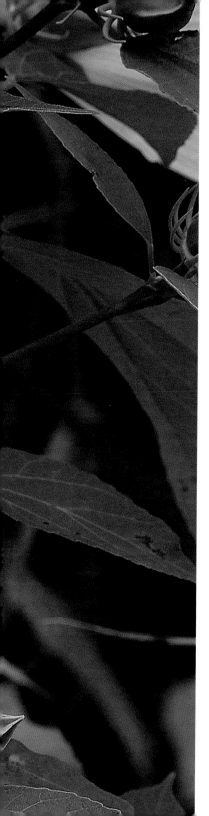

Reaching heights of about seven feet, the marsh hibiscus is a very common summer wildflower on the Eastern Shore. Also called rose mallow or swamp cotton – it's in the same family as cotton – the flowers of this showy wildflower are either creamy white or brilliant pink, but always with a dark crimson center. The marsh hibiscus flourishes on tidal freshwater marshes and along the edges of salt marshes. The smaller seashore mallow is much more tolerant of saline conditions. The peak flowering periods for marsh hibiscus are from late July to early September. Its dazzling color adds a nice complement to the emerald green hue of the marsh.

During a partly cloudy day at Eastern Neck National Wildlife Refuge, I combed the refuge's main road in search of a nice composition of marsh hibiscus. Waiting for the sun to become obscured by the passing clouds so a more even lighting would fall on the composition, I used my 70-180mm macro lens to compose this image. The clouds were moving rather slowly, so it took a couple of hours to capture just the right image. The heat and humidity added a challenge to my intentions, but once the clouds blocked the sun, I diligently went back to work photographing this icon of the Eastern Shore summer season.

Right: Marsh hibiscus and narrow-leafed cattail, Dorchester County, Maryland.

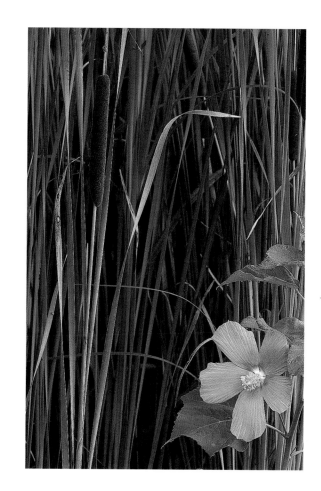

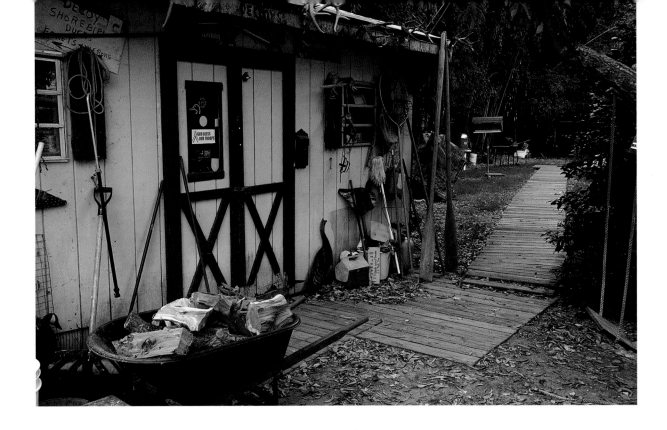

For more than 70 years, Chincoteague has been home for Cork and Lola McGee, true "teaguers" in every sense of the word. With the exception of their wedding in 1950 at Pocomoke City on the mainland, the McGees' lives have centered on Chincoteague. No two finer people can be found on the island, much less the entire Eastern Shore, but it is Cork's exceptional skill at carving pieces of basswood into works of art that brings people from all over the country to their home on McGee Lane.

Cork is a world-class wood carver. From canvasback decoys to carvings of flying shorebirds to hand-crafted life-sized great blue herons, Cork's eloquent creations of the island's bird life stirs memories in every individual so honored to own one of them. Cork's carvings embody the unpretentious beauty of nature's design. His work is a celebration of the creatures roaming the marshes, woodlands, and beaches of his beloved island. While a life-long hunter and fisherman, Cork began his wood-carving career in 1957. As word spread about his work, Cork eventually made the transition from waterman to full-time artist.

Lola inspects every carving Cork produces and for much of the time, the very first carving of a species goes to her. The customer will often have to settle for the second edition.

Above: Cork McGee's wood-carving shop.

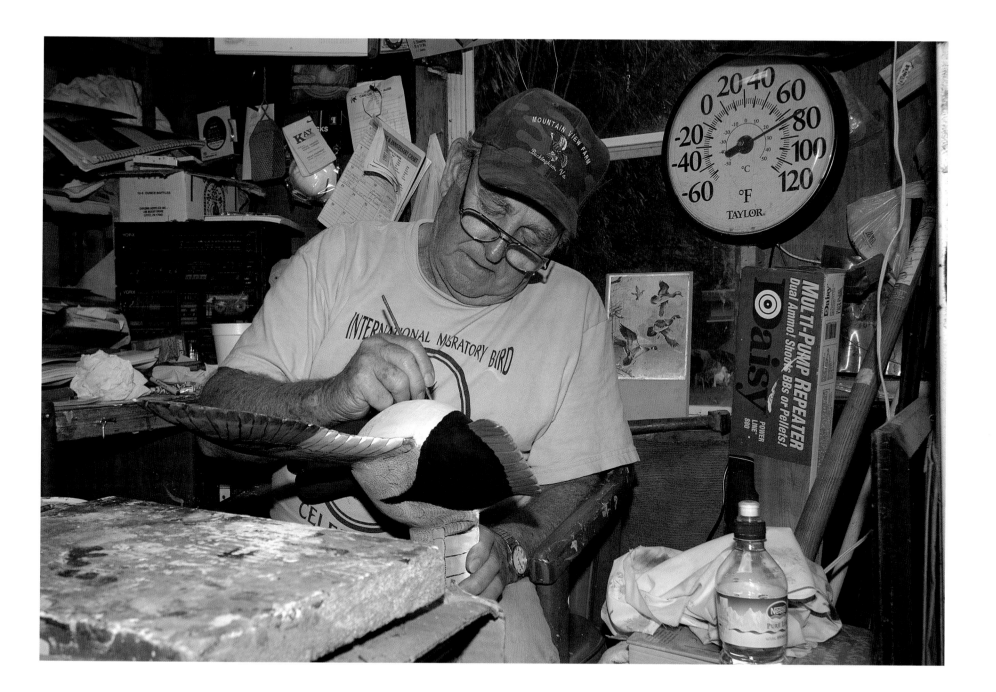

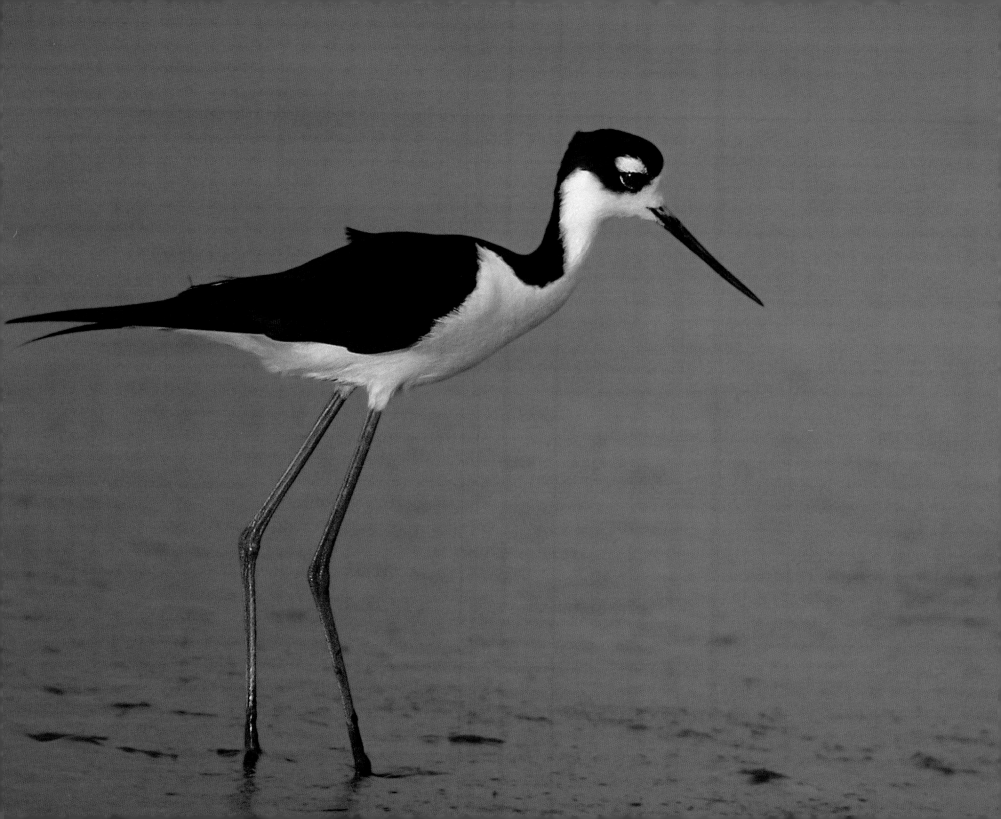

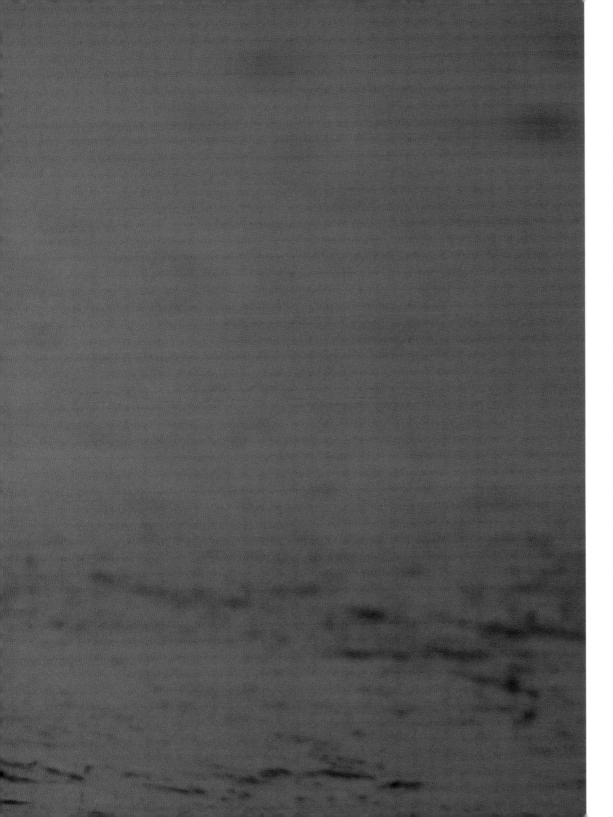

Birders from around the world meet each spring on the Eastern Shore to witness the amazing shorebird gathering that occurs here. Depending upon the weather patterns, the region's exposed mud and tidal flats can harbor thousands of shorebirds, each bird frantically feeding to refuel their depleted energy reserves for their continued journey north. A wondrous sight during this time of the year are the hundreds and thousands of shorebirds in one flock, flying in unison over the marsh, searching for another exposed flat upon which to land and feed.

Bombay Hook National Wildlife Refuge in Delaware is one of the world's top shorebird watching destinations. May is the prime month for the spring shorebird migration at the refuge, while August and September are peak for the fall migration season. During the summer months, human visitation to the refuge is practically zero because of the amazing concentrations of mosquitoes, horseflies, and other winged biting insects. If you go to the refuge at this time of the year, be prepared for an onslaught of hungry aerial invertebrates.

One of the refuge's shorebird specialties is the elegant black-necked stilt. With a slender black and white frame perched on thin red legs, the stilt is a dramatic departure from the usual chunky, brown-plumaged shorebirds that are normally encountered here. The stilt also nests on the refuge and can be quite vocal to any intruder who dares disturb its nest.

This stilt was photographed along the refuge's auto-tour route one spring morning. The stilt was feeding along an exposed mudflat. I used a 600mm telephoto lens with a 1.4x extender to capture the image while I was still in my truck. Just enough of the sun's rays painted the bird so that a small catchlight was captured in its ruby-red eyes.

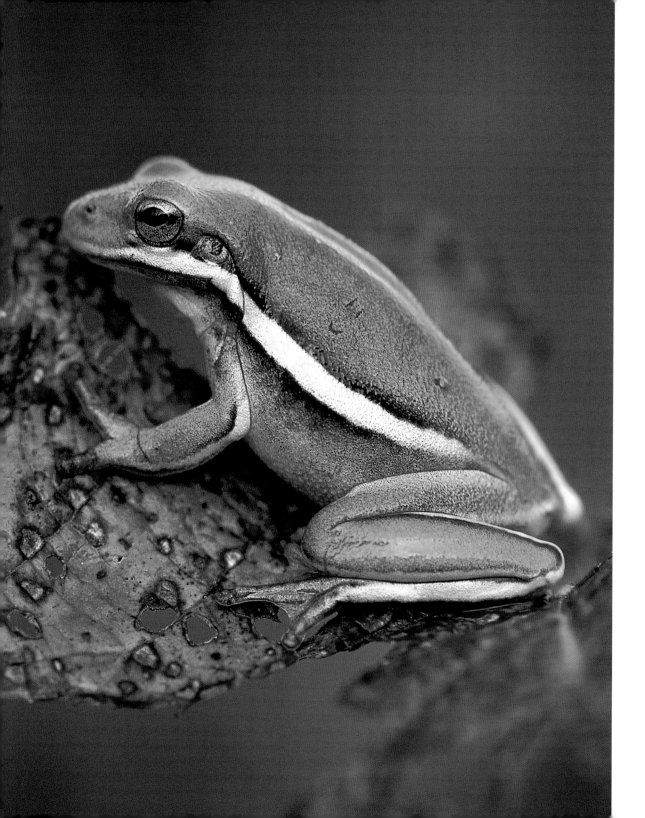

During the early hours of an October morning on the Eastern Shore, I was exploring a bramble-filled hedgerow near the headquarters of Blackwater National Wildlife Refuge, which is located along the eastern shore of the Chesapeake Bay. The refuge protects an extraordinary diversity of life, including the endangered bald eagle and Delmarva fox squirrel. While each season offers its own unique assortment of wild critters, the fall season is the best time to see thousands of waterfowl on the refuge's wetlands.

This particular autumn morning greeted me with layers of fog floating just above the ground. The air had a definite chill and a heavy coat of dew covered every leaf and stem of vegetation in the hedgerow. Looking down into the weedy growth, I discovered this small green tree frog firmly attached to a blackberry stem. Because of the cool temperature, the frog wasn't going to move much. Using a 200mm micro lens firmly attached to a tripod, I got on my knees and photographed the frog from its point of view. More than an hour and several rolls of film later, I finally stop photographing. Just outside this composition, a large praying mantis was also waiting for the sun to warm its body. The simple act of noticing helps to discover these hidden jewels within the natural world. The Eastern Shore is chocked-full of these veiled surprises.

During the early morning and late evening hours at Blackwater National Wildlife Refuge, the edges of the roads and trails become favorite feeding spots for the eastern cottontail. Skittish at first blush, cottontails can become very accommodating to a nature photographer who takes the time to "work" the subject.

While patience is an important attribute to have as a nature photographer, the ability to adjust one's perspective in photographing wildlife can greatly add to a successful shoot as well. By simply photographing from the "eye-level" of the creature, you can not only get a more powerful composition, but the animal becomes a little more tolerant of the human's presence. When anticipating such a possibility, it's wise to plan ahead and lower the tripod to at least knee level. This perspective yields a much more pleasing straight on composition.

Using these very techniques, I was successful at sharing some early morning light with this hungry rabbit on the auto-tour route at Blackwater. Starting at a respectable distance from the cottontail, I slowly made my way – on my knees – to the feeding critter. Often times, at the moment of initial panic, the rabbit would dash back into the safety of the road-side shrubbery. But eventually, it made its way back out to feed. Within minutes the rabbit became tolerant of me and I was able to photograph it for several minutes.

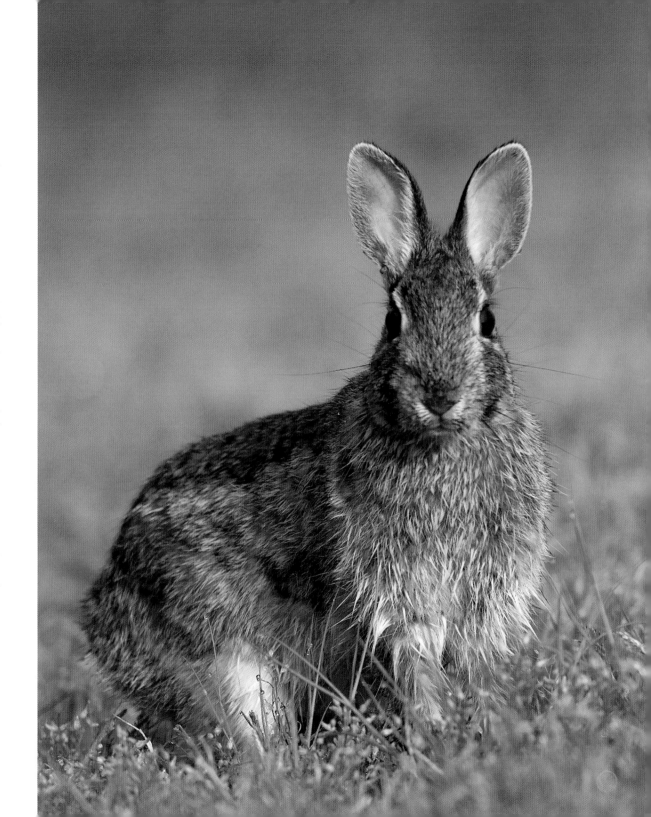

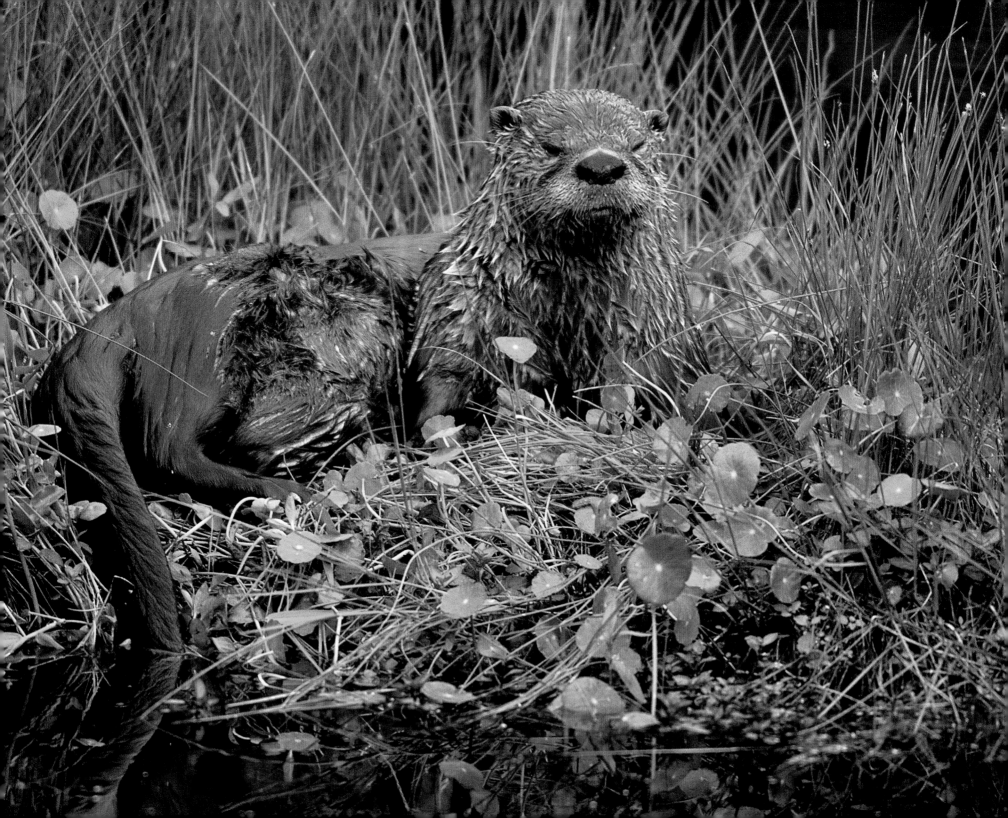

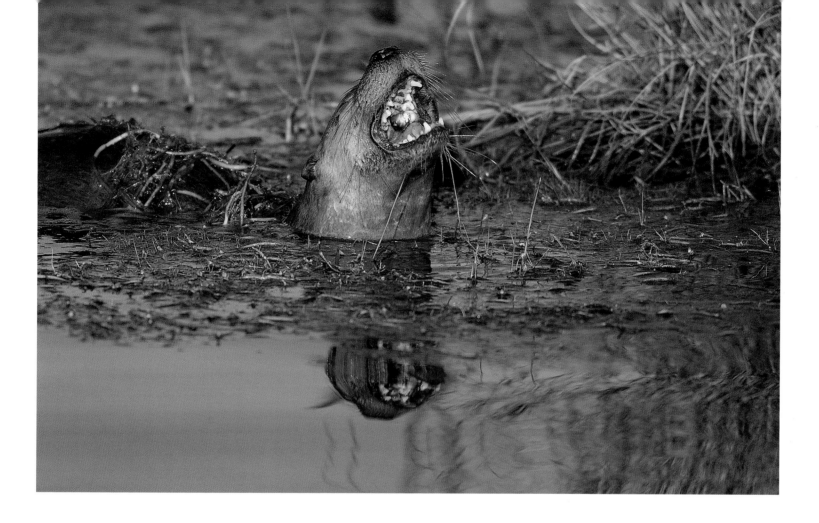

The river otter is often a very secretive creature of the Eastern Shore. Frequenting the freshwater and brackish marshes, this elusive mammal feeds on a variety of aquatic life, from frogs and crayfish, to crabs and fish. To have an opportunity to watch these playful creatures is one of the highlights for a nature lover exploring this region.

During a spring nature photography workshop at Chincoteague National Wildlife Refuge, my students and I were intent on photographing a Delmarva fox squirrel across a ditch along Beach Road. We were so entranced with the squirrel that we did not realize a river otter was cleaning itself on the opposite side of the road. A passerby stopped and told us to look behind us. Imagine our surprise – and delight – when we saw a lone river otter on the grassy bank along Black Duck Pool.

We quickly turned our attention to photographing the otter as it preened. The otter provided us about ten minutes of uninhibited photographic opportunities before sliding back into the water and swimming upstream. Since that day I always check the ditches along the roads at the refuge for signs of these wonderful critters . . . and I always look behind me after I photograph what is in front of me.

Above: A river otter eats a frog.

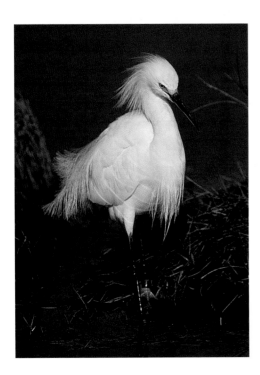

The snowy egret was at one time near extinction as a result of the once thriving millinery (feather) trade. The egret's long filamentous plumes on its back were highly prized for women's hats. Through the efforts of concerned naturalists, citizens, and one president – Theodore Roosevelt – these birds along with other wading birds were saved from near annihilation.

Sanctuaries were established and President Roosevelt, through the stroke of a pen, established several national wildlife refuges to protect the breeding areas of wading birds such as the snowy. The subsequent passage of the Migratory Bird Treaty Act also helped to stem the tide in the bird's favor. Our marshes and wetlands would be a lesser place without these magnificent birds and their cohorts such as the great blue heron, little blue heron, and great egret.

While exploring the northern reaches of Chincoteague Island, I followed this feisty snowy egret feeding during a most pleasant spring morning. The egret was using its gold-clad colored feet to stir the mud, raking its feet back and forth across the water to scare up small fish and crustaceans. The bird was too intent on feeding to notice me, but my 600mm telephoto lens provided a nice safe distance between the egret and me. The thought of how these beautiful birds were nearly wiped from the planet, gave me pause that morning to think how empty our world would be without them.

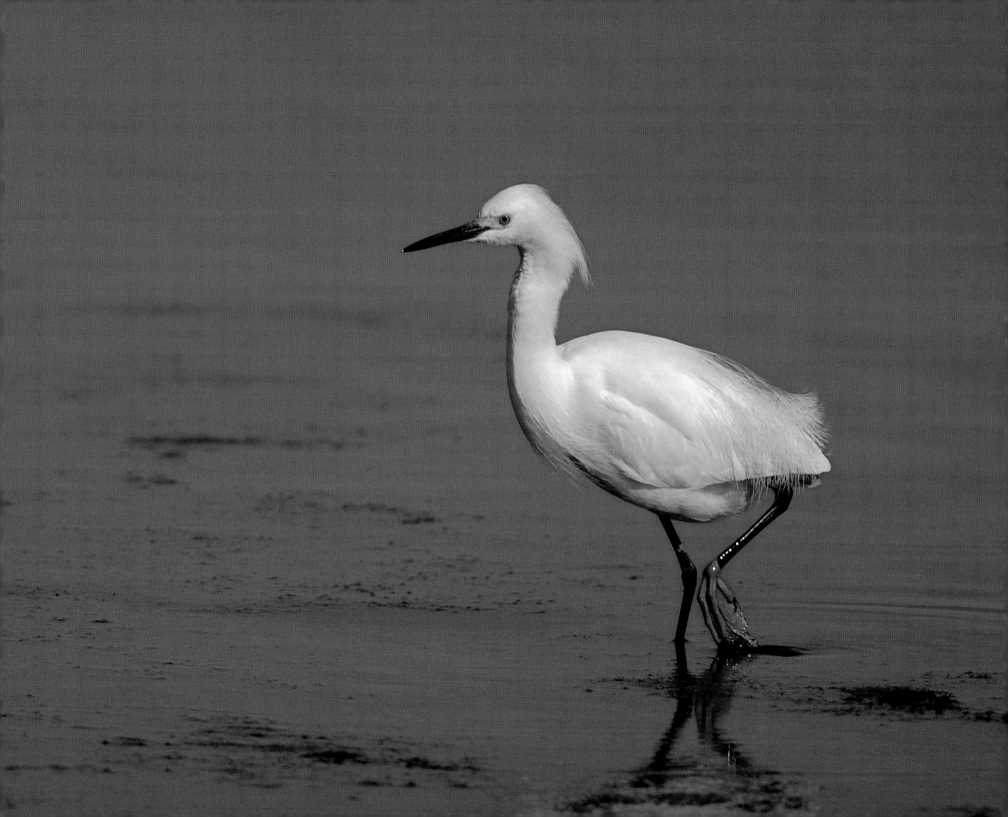

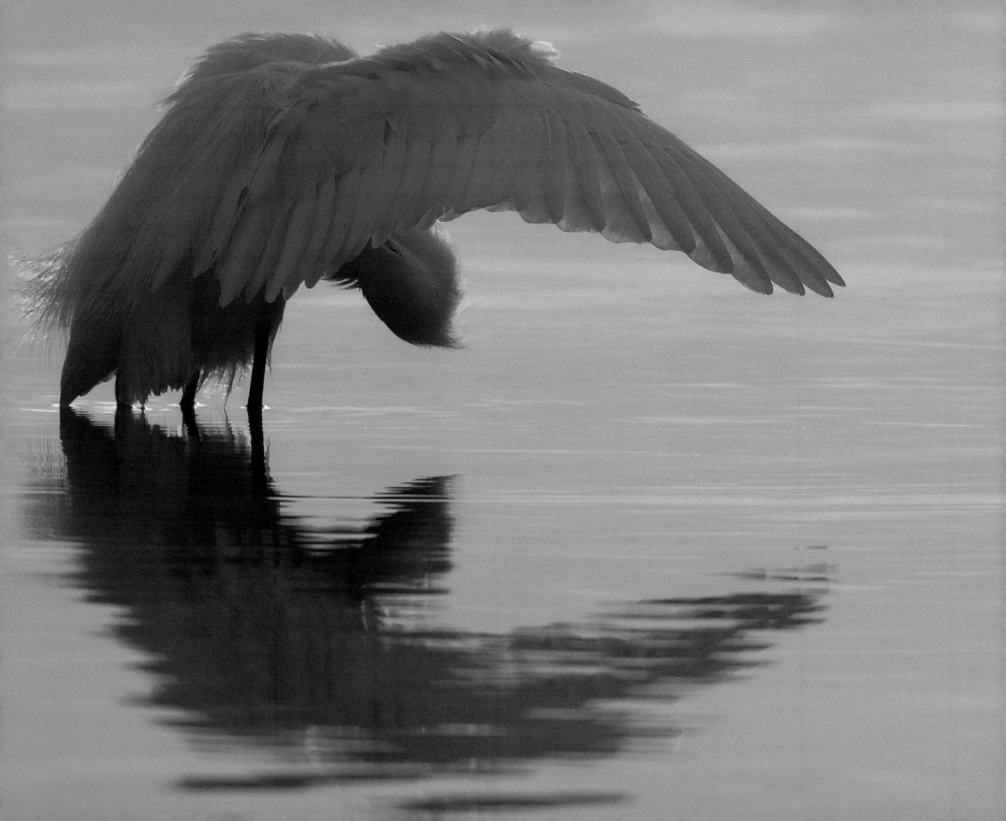

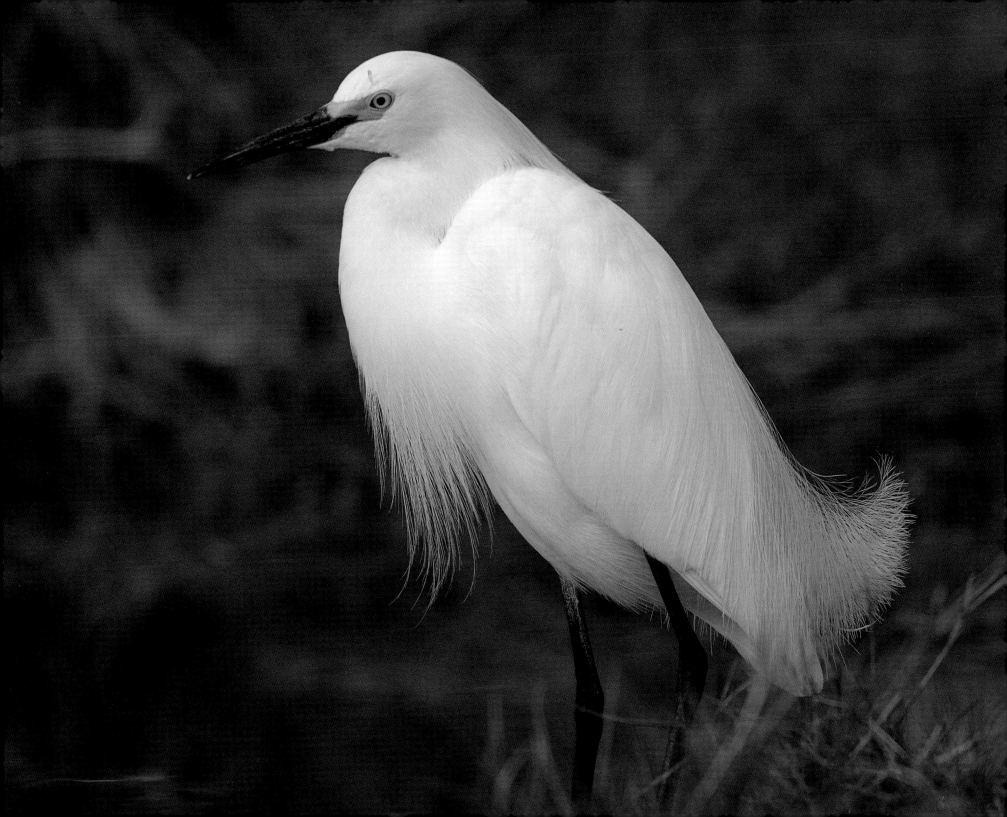

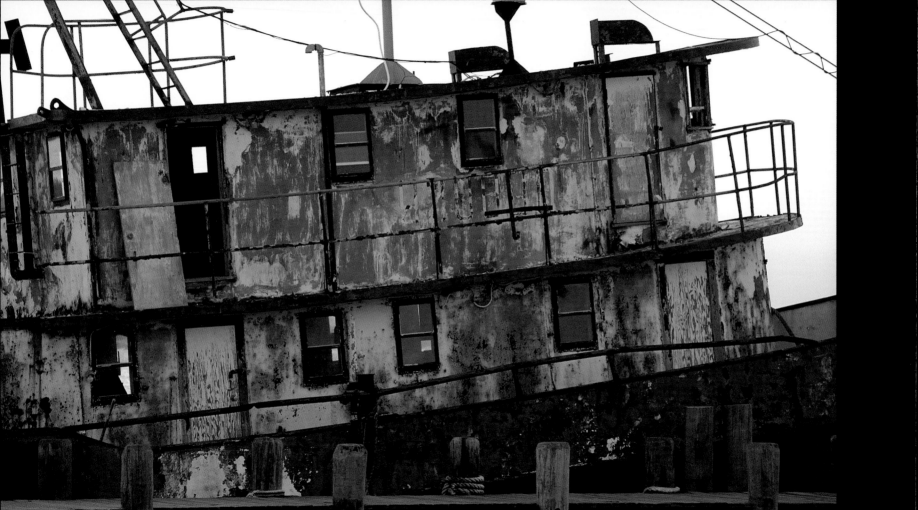

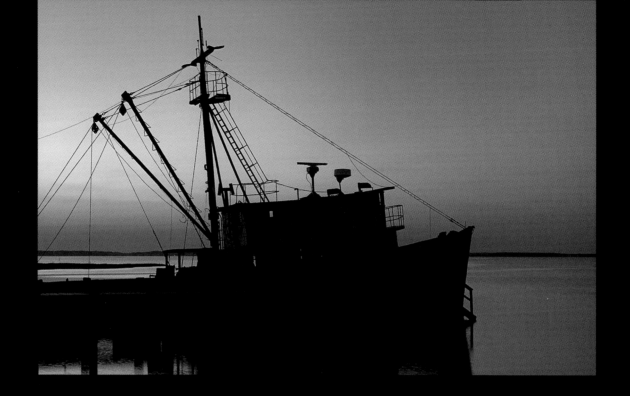

This old fishing boat stays moored along the docks on Chincoteague's bayside. Every time I see this vessel, I'm reminded of the proud fishing heritage that once made Chincoteague a thriving center for the seafood industry.

By the mid-1800s, the seafood industry was the primary economic driver for most island residents. The major northeastern cities of Baltimore, New York, and Philadelphia provided a steady stream of business for the island's famous oysters. Along the island's western shore, processing plants and shucking houses prepared the oysters for shipment. Later, in the early 1900s, after the oyster population declined, the island's seafood businesses included harvests of clams, crabs, and fish.

While seafood harvesting – primarily for scallops – still plays a major role on Chincoteague, the primary economic force these days is tourism. The completion of the bridge linking the island of Chincoteague with Chincoteague National Wildlife Refuge and Assateague Island National Seashore changed the character of the island forever.

Today, Chincoteague's population of 3500 suddenly swells tenfold during the summer season. Annually, Chincoteague plays host to more than 1.5 million visitors with most of the visitation occurring from June to August.

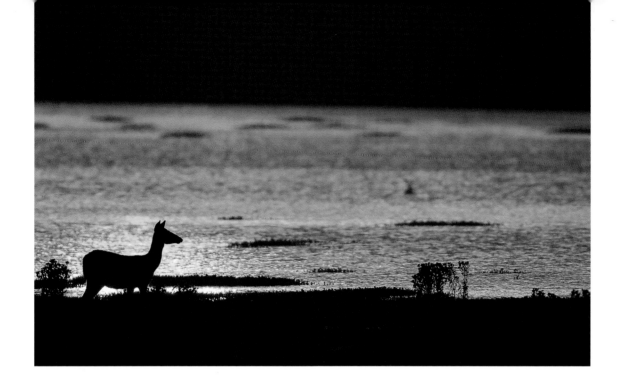

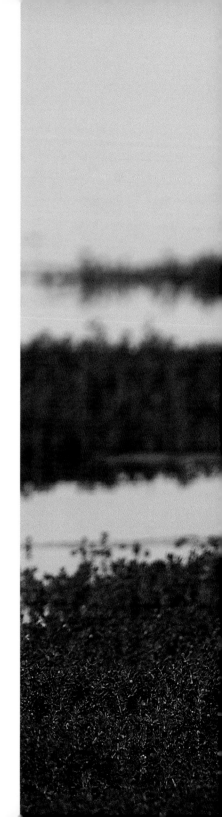

During one mild early fall afternoon at Chincoteague National Wildlife Refuge, I decided to explore the refuge's wildlife drive. The temperatures were warm enough to enjoy this autumn day, but still cool enough to keep the mosquitoes down to a manageable bite level. A steady and gentle coastal breeze also prevented the mosquitoes from engaging in a full frontal attack.

With the sun setting, I positioned myself near Black Duck Pool, hoping to capture the sun setting over the marsh. While getting ready, I looked behind me and saw this white-tailed deer feeding along the edge of the marsh. The spike buck still had some velvet on its antlers. The lighting was low and perfectly painted onto the marsh, providing a warm glow to the deer's coat.

The buck continued to feed in the marsh and surprisingly, move closer to me. Using a 600mm telephoto lens, I stayed put and kept photographing the buck until it eventually made its way to the edge of the marsh, finally disappearing into the forest.

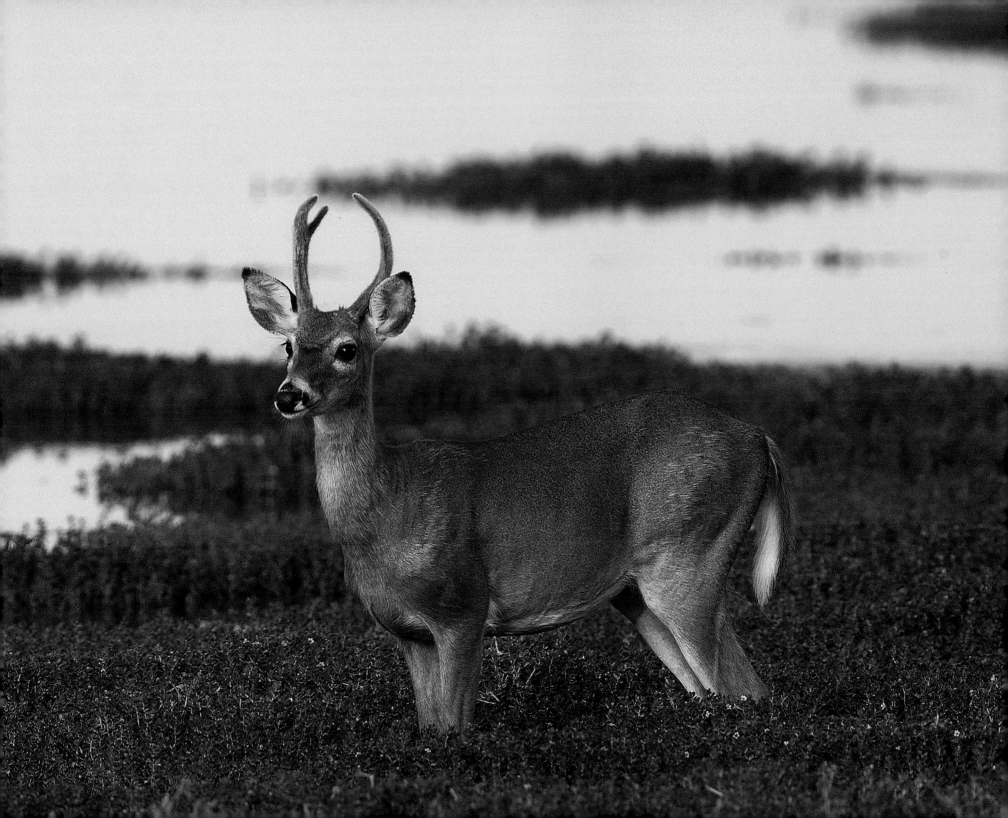

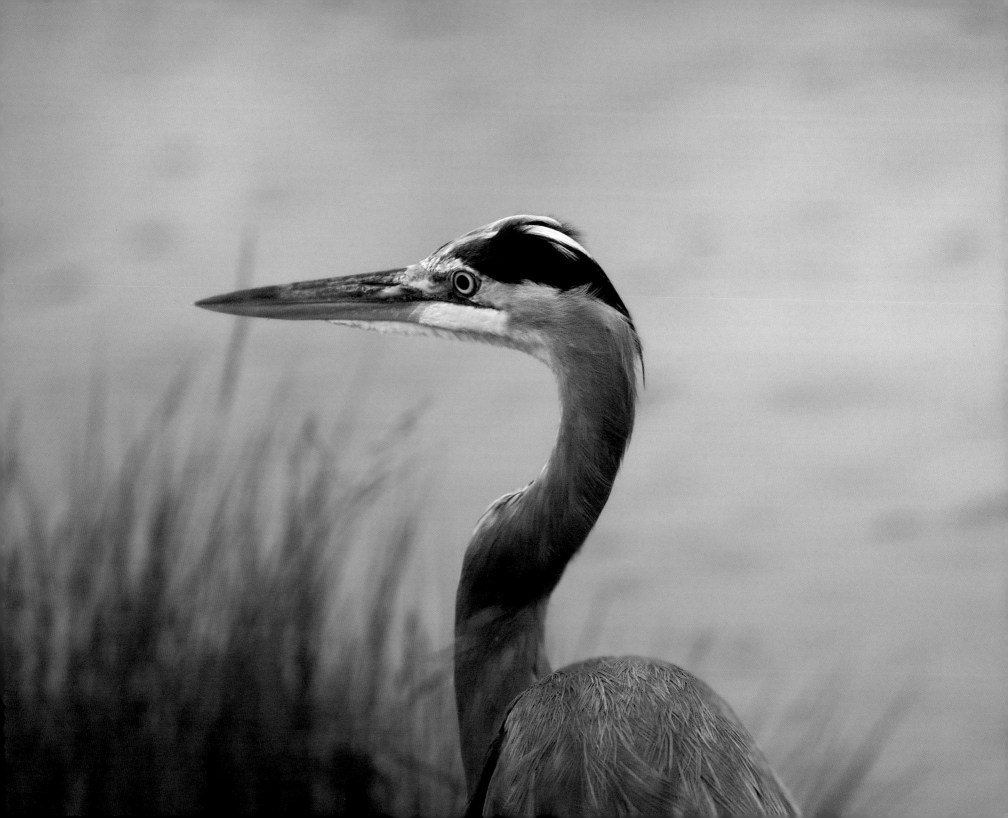

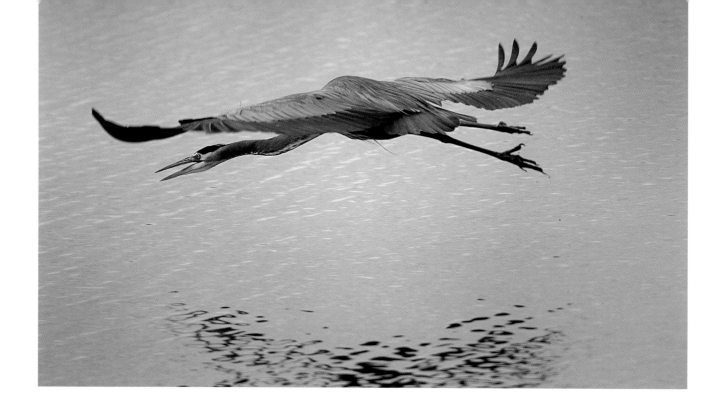

Blue crab and oyster notwithstanding, the great blue is probably the most recognized feathered creature most visitors see and think about when describing the nature of the Eastern Shore. While more common along the region's bayside, these graceful long-legged wading birds can be seen in just about every nook and cranny of the Eastern Shore. But there is no better location to see the great blues than in the marshes surrounding Blackwater National Wildlife Refuge. On some days, it's not uncommon to see more than 20 of these wading birds in one wetland pool.

This great blue was feeding along the refuge's auto-tour road during an early spring evening. As daylight faded and the wind gusts became more forceful, the heron took flight and landed across a borrow ditch. Nestled among the taller reeds and cattails that protected the bird from the wind, the heron remained steadfast. I slowly made my way to the edge of the borrow ditch directly across from the heron. I was able to spend several minutes photographing this magnificent bird.

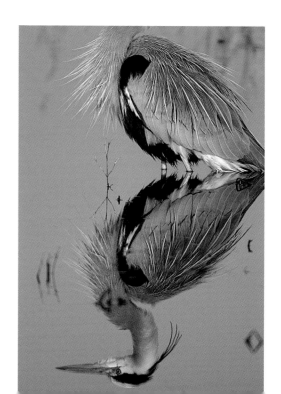

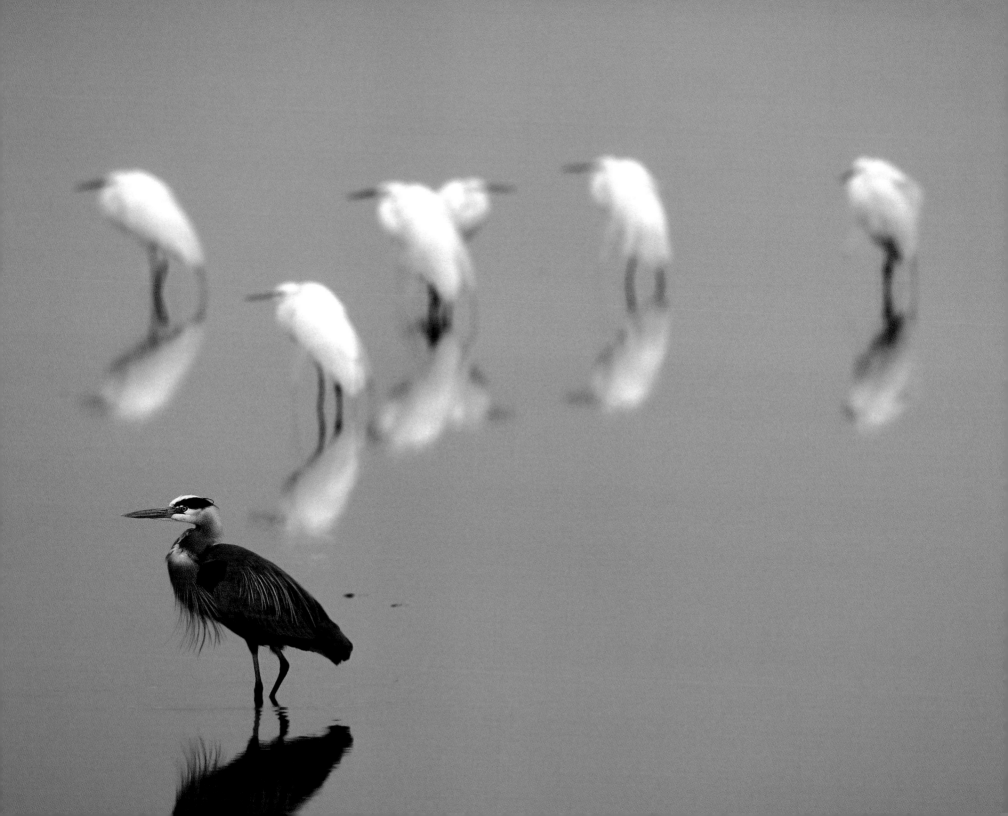

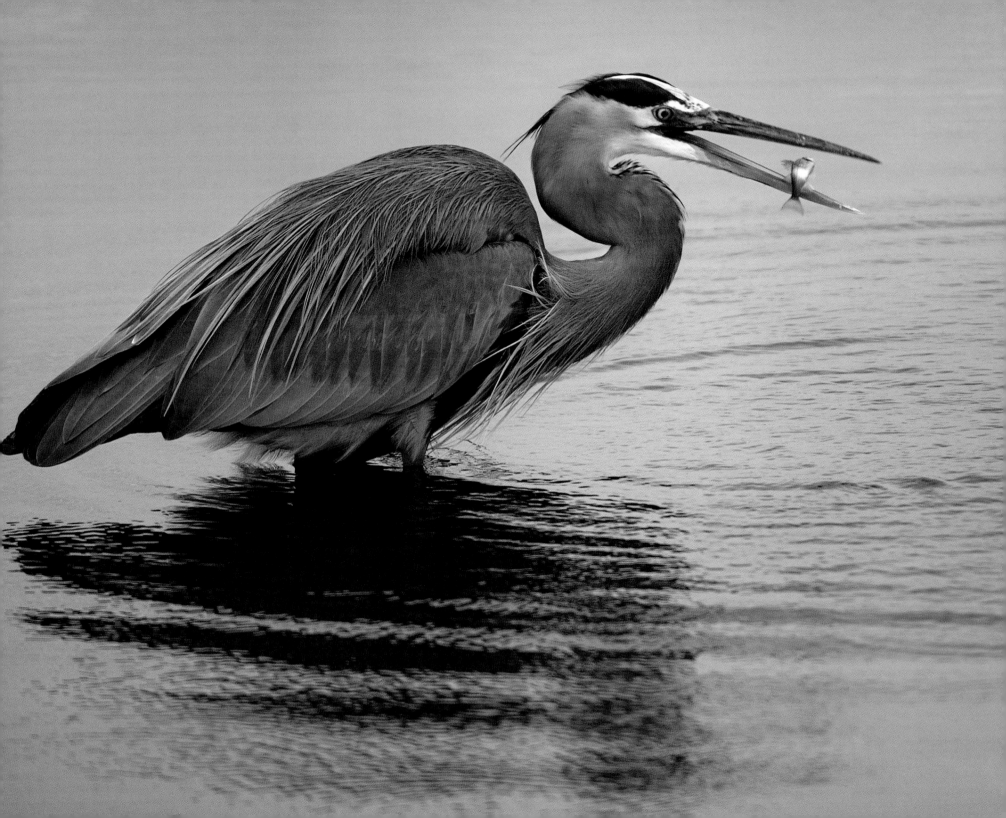

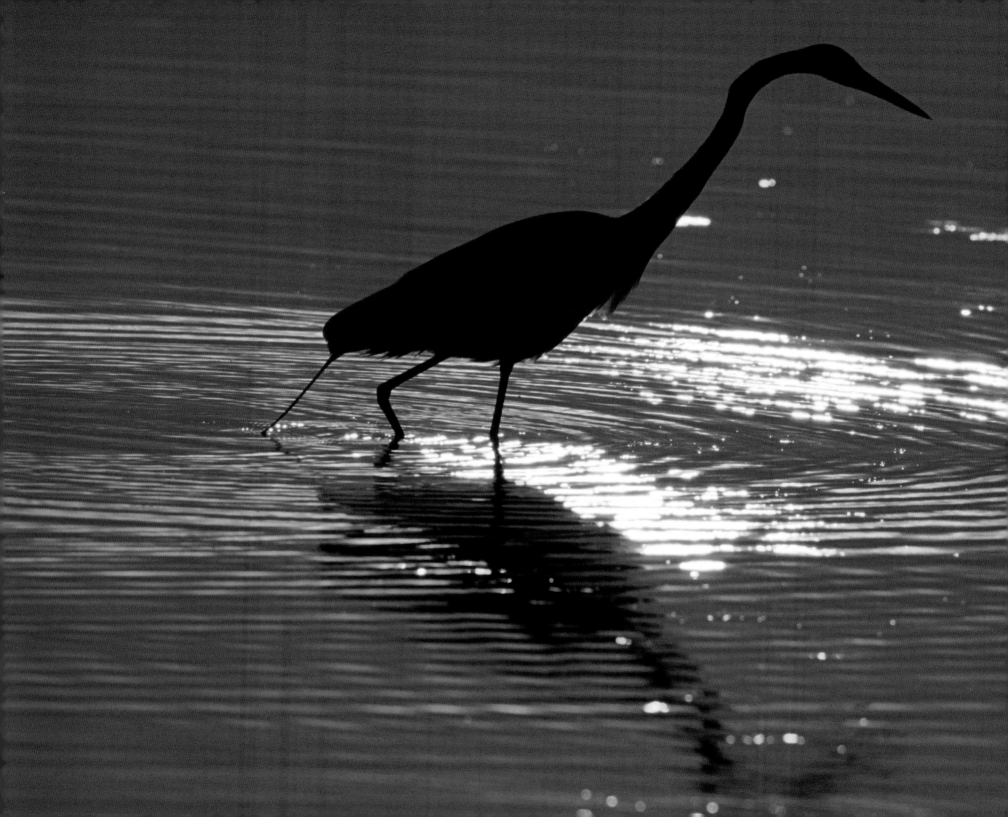

As one of the crown jewels of the National Wildlife Refuge System, Chincoteague National Wildlife Refuge is a sanctuary among a sea of humanity. Protecting more than 14,000 acres of salt marsh, loblolly forests, and coastal beaches, Chincoteague is a world-renowned birding site. More than 320 bird species have been recorded here. Every season brings something new and birders from around the world flock to this Eastern Shore refuge to add birds to their life list.

For wading birds, Chincoteague is hard to beat. The wetlands provide feeding, resting, and nesting habitats for a variety of long-legged waders including great and snowy egrets, great blue, green, tricolored, and little blue herons, and the secretive black-crowned and yellow-crowned night-herons. During tidal exchange periods, at times more than 100 wading birds will congregate at these places to feed on the fish as they travel up and down the channels.

This great egret was feeding in Little Toms Cove during one early spring morning. The concentric rings were formed as the egret plunged its bill into the water for a fish. Eventually, the egret prevailed in grabbing something for breakfast.

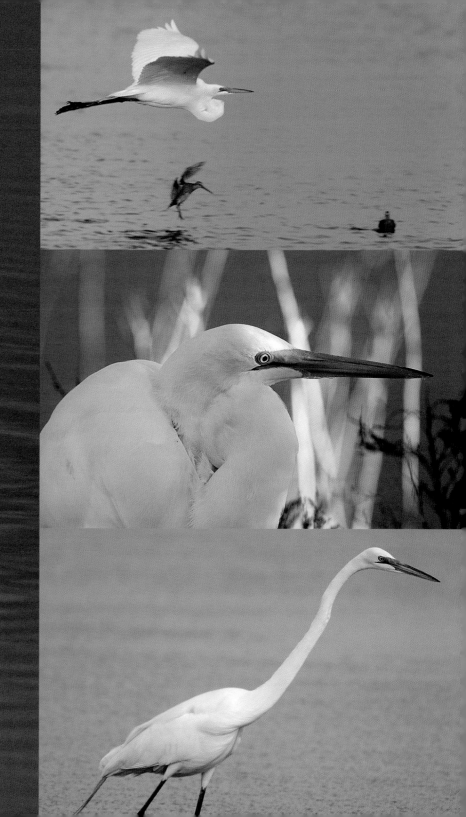

Assateague Island National Seashore is one of the premier locations along the Mid-Atlantic seaboard to collect seashells. Exploring the beach after a storm will usually result in a productive shelling trip. "Northeasterners" wash the shells on shore, but if the storm is strong, the shells may be pummeled into fragments. A gentler southeasterner storm, however, results in the shells becoming beached without much wear and tear. Regardless of the season, the best time to find shells is during low tides and immediately after a storm has passed through.

One crisp autumn morning while exploring the southern reaches of Assateague Island, I discovered clusters of shells just above the tide line. The primary species were quahogs (the highly-prized edible clam) and Atlantic bay scallops (another delectable culinary delight).

I collected several of the shells, spread them out on the sandy beach, and proceeded photographing them. A diffuser was used to help reduce contrast in the scene. With pelicans and oystercatchers flying overhead and a soft ocean breeze filling the air with a wonderful coastal fragrance, I was in no hurry to leave.

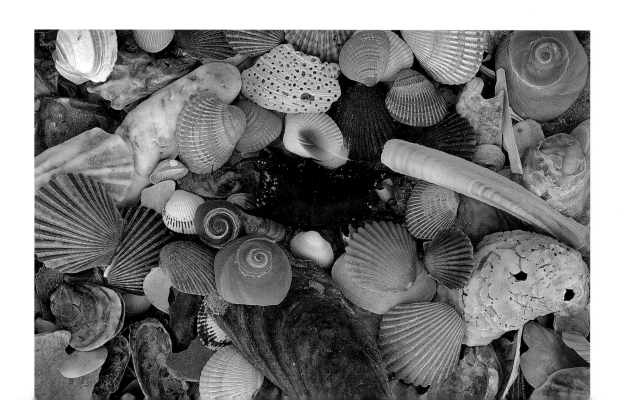

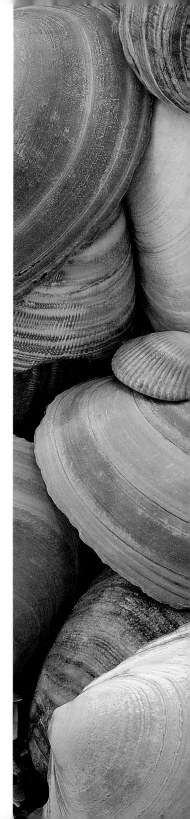

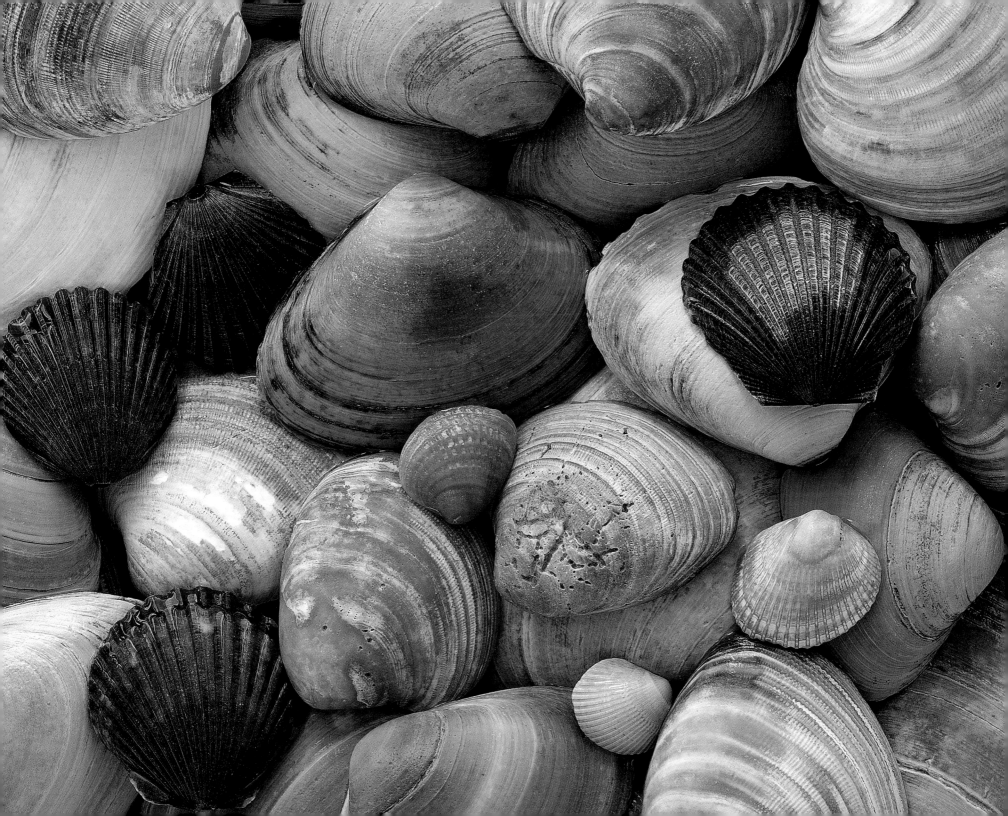

Only two of the more than 400 species of true toads in the world occur on the Eastern Shore: American and Fowlers. The Eastern spade foot and narrow-mouthed toads are also found here, but they are not true toads since they lack dry warty skin, horizontal pupils, and parotoid glands behind the eyes. Female toads are also much larger than the males. Of the two toad species, only the Fowlers toad occurs on coastal barrier islands. They prefer the sandy soil much more than the American.

Peak breeding for the Fowlers toad occurs from mid-April through May during warm, rainy nights. Females deposit thousands of eggs – some speculate more than 8,000 eggs are laid by a single female – in two gelatinous strands. By late May, hundreds upon hundreds of tiny toads can be encountered along hiking trails and along wetland edges.

While leading a spring nature photographing workshop at Chincoteague National Wildlife Refuge, my students and I decided to hike the refuge's Woodland Trail in hopes of photographing the endangered Delmarva fox squirrel. Instead, we discovered hundreds of Fowlers toads hopping across the trail. With my belly on the sand and a 200mm macro lens on a tripod, I spent the mid-morning photographing the toads. The tick season had not kicked into high gear, so I was spared the agony of picking off these blood-sucking invertebrates.

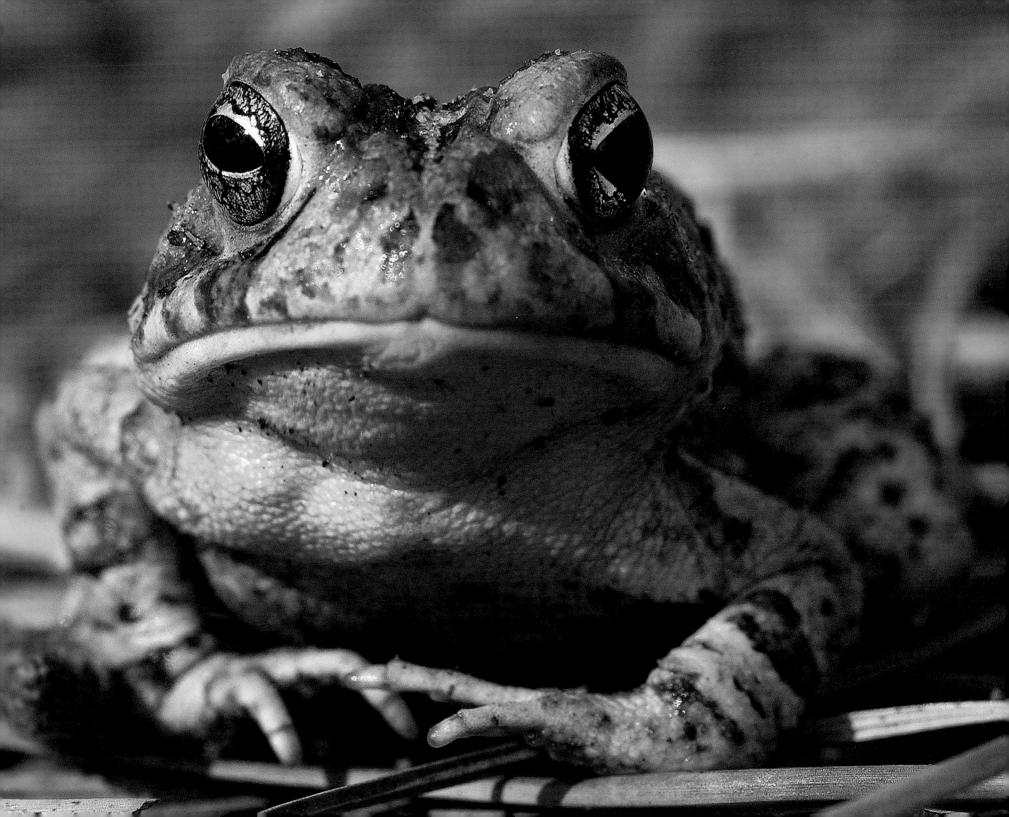

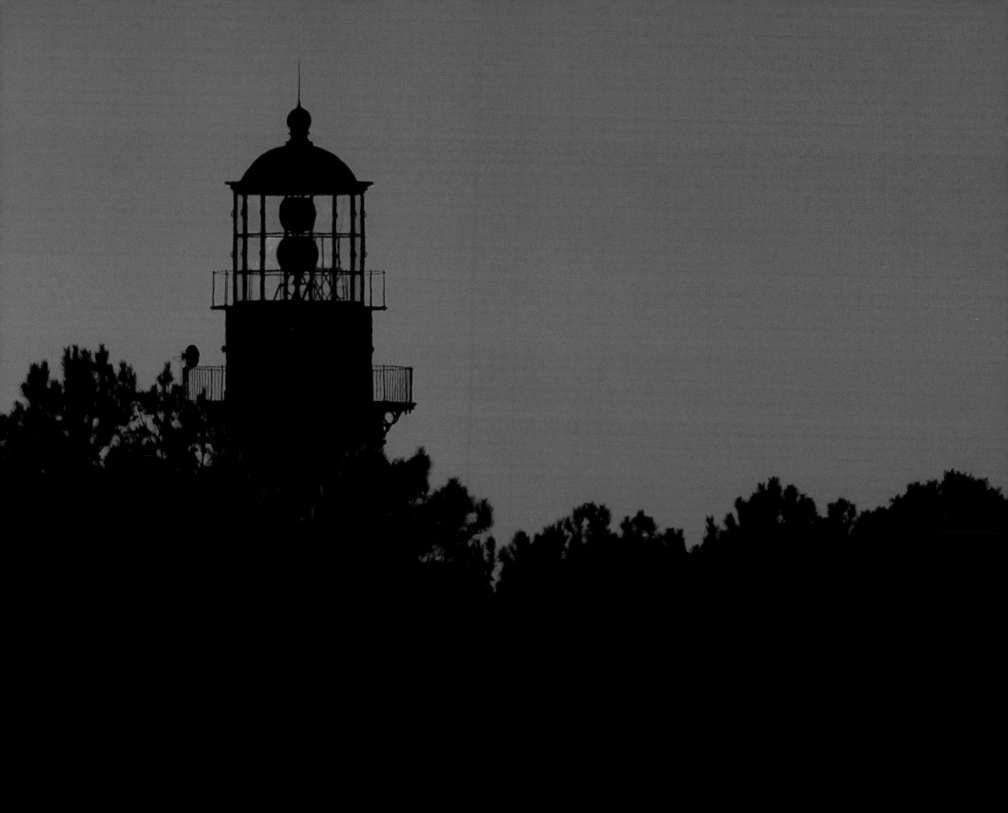

The first lighthouse on Assateague Island was constructed in 1883 to help ships navigate through the dangerous shoals offshore. Attempts to build a taller lighthouse were stymied by the advent of the Civil War, but eventually the new 142 foot structure was finished in 1867. The new lighthouse was constructed on a sand ridge. Due to sand deposition over the years, the lighthouse is now situated more inland, nearer to the bayside of the island.

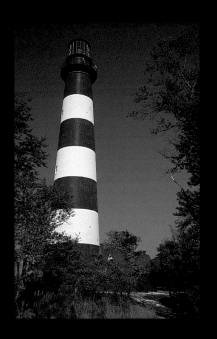

The lighthouse was operated by a keeper until 1932 when an electric lamp was installed. Ownership of the lighthouse transferred from the U.S. Coast Guard to the U.S. Fish and Wildlife Service in 2004. The lighthouse remains an active navigational aide and is now listed on the National Register of Historic Places.

While most photographers opt to photograph the lighthouse along the sandy paths leading to it, I decided to try something different. While photographing some white-tailed deer along the edge of the refuge wildlife drive, I noticed the lighthouse towering above the loblolly pines. Amidst a throng of aggressive mosquitoes, I used my 600mm telephoto lens to capture this isolated scenic of the lighthouse silhouetted against a dramatic blood-red September sky.

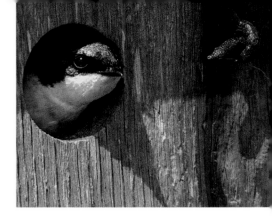

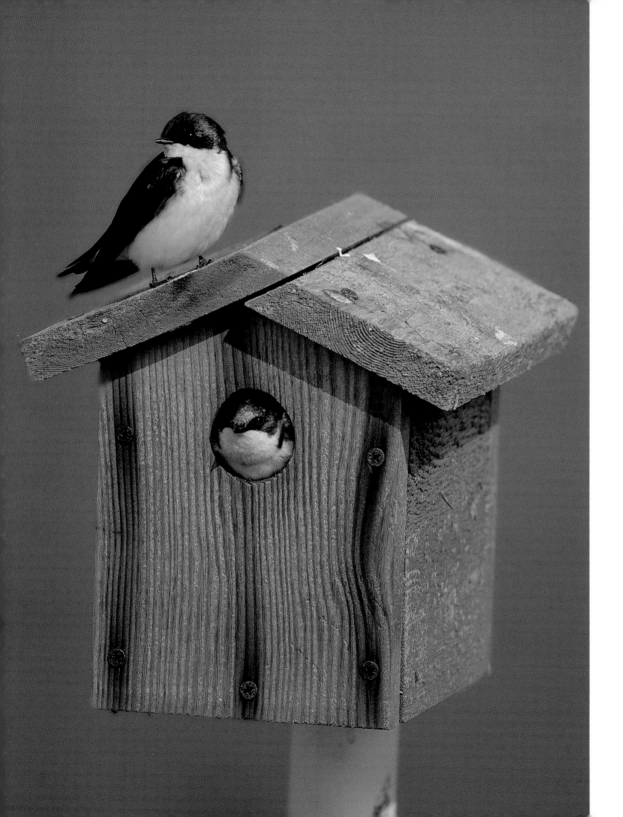

In North America eighty-five species of birds are classified as cavity nesters. These are species that depend upon holes in dead or decadent trees for nest sites. Species such as woodpeckers create their own cavities, while many other species, including the tree swallow, are dependent upon existing cavities for their nest sites. In the event that natural cavities are not available, tree swallows and other species will readily accept nest boxes.

Tree swallows are one of the early spring migrants to the Eastern Shore and they are not too particular about the nest box they use. Bluebird boxes and purple martin houses are frequently occupied by tree swallows, but their preference is for nest boxes located on or near a water source. Because of the decline in natural cavities in their preferred habitat, tree swallows are becoming even more dependent upon nest boxes.

This pair of tree swallows had taken up residence at a nest box located in a freshwater marsh along the Marsh Trail at Chincoteague National Wildlife Refuge. One adult stood vigil on top of the box, while the other adult incubated the eggs inside. Tree swallows are not as dependent upon insects as a food source as other swallows species are. Berries from wax myrtle and bayberry are favored plant foods for these winged aerial acrobats. Often times, as in the case of the tree swallow, it pays to be flexible.

Diminutive in size and secretive in nature, the eastern screech owl is one of the Eastern Shore's most fascinating creatures. Occurring in two color phases – red and gray – the owl's eerie quavering trill filters through the night air and send chills up the spine of anyone not familiar with its call. The owl also has a secondary song described as a long single trill, that the male uses to advertise a nest site or to attract a mate.

Primarily a nocturnal species, this lone screech owl was discovered one afternoon while hiking along a trail through the piney woodlands at Chincoteague National Wildlife Refuge. Silently perched on a loblolly tree branch, the little owl didn't seem too alarmed by my presence. The screech owl is a cavity nester, choosing abandoned woodpecker holes for its nest site. But this owl seemed content to soak up the spring sunshine. For nearly an hour, I photographed the owl with my 600mm lens. With the sun facing me, I used flash to fill in the shadows.

The next morning I decided to hike the same trail just to see if the owl was still there. And there it was, perched almost exactly on the same location of the same branch as the day before. I spent another hour and several more rolls of film photographing the owl.

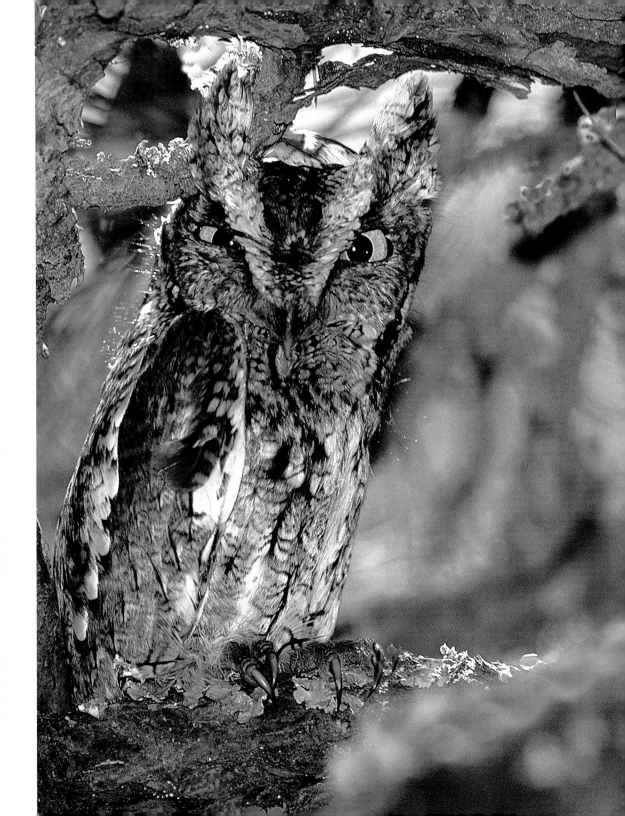

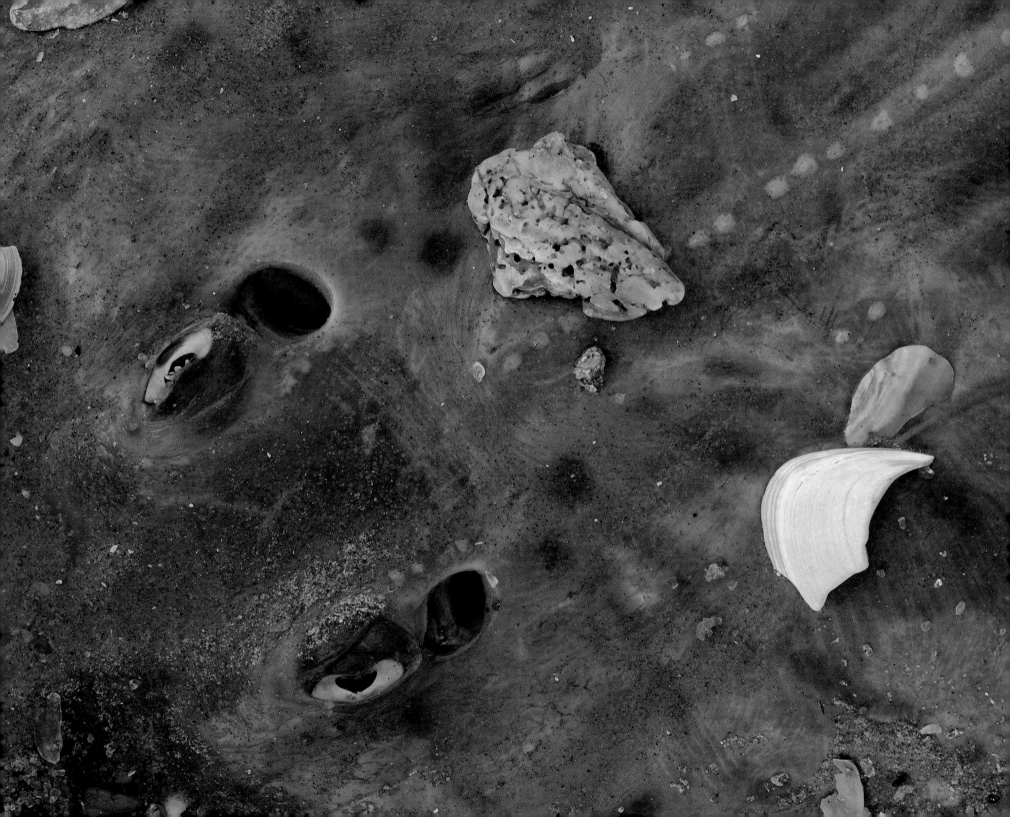

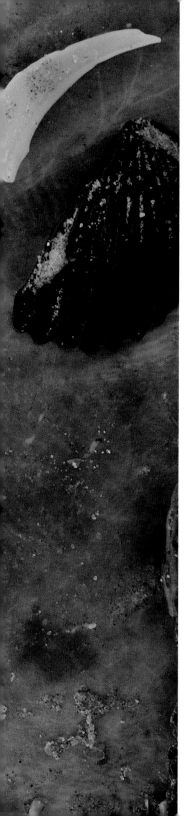

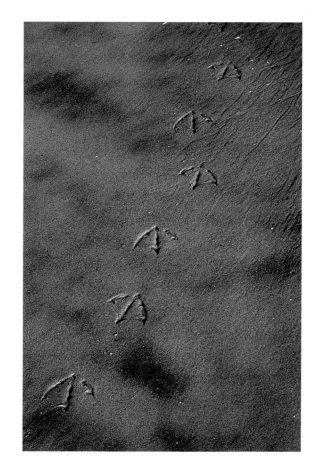

The stingray is one marine creature most beachgoers would prefer not to encounter at any time. Commonly found in the shallow coastal waters along the Atlantic coast, the stingray spends the majority of its time partially buried in sand, often moving only with the movement of the tide. The stingray's spine is fashioned with serrated edges and a sharp point, and while it is not an aggressive animal, its spine can cause a very painful injury on the unfortunate human who steps on it. On rare occasions, the injury can be lethal.

I discovered this stranded stingray on the beach at Assateague Island National Seashore in Virginia while I was photographing seashells that had washed onshore after a storm the previous night. Knowing the ray's spine can still inflict pain even when the animal is dead, I carefully positioned my camera over the ray to get a bird's eye view of the ray with the shells scattered on its back. Despite its reputation, the stingray is one of the ocean's most remarkable creatures.

Right: Gull tracks in the sand at Assateague.

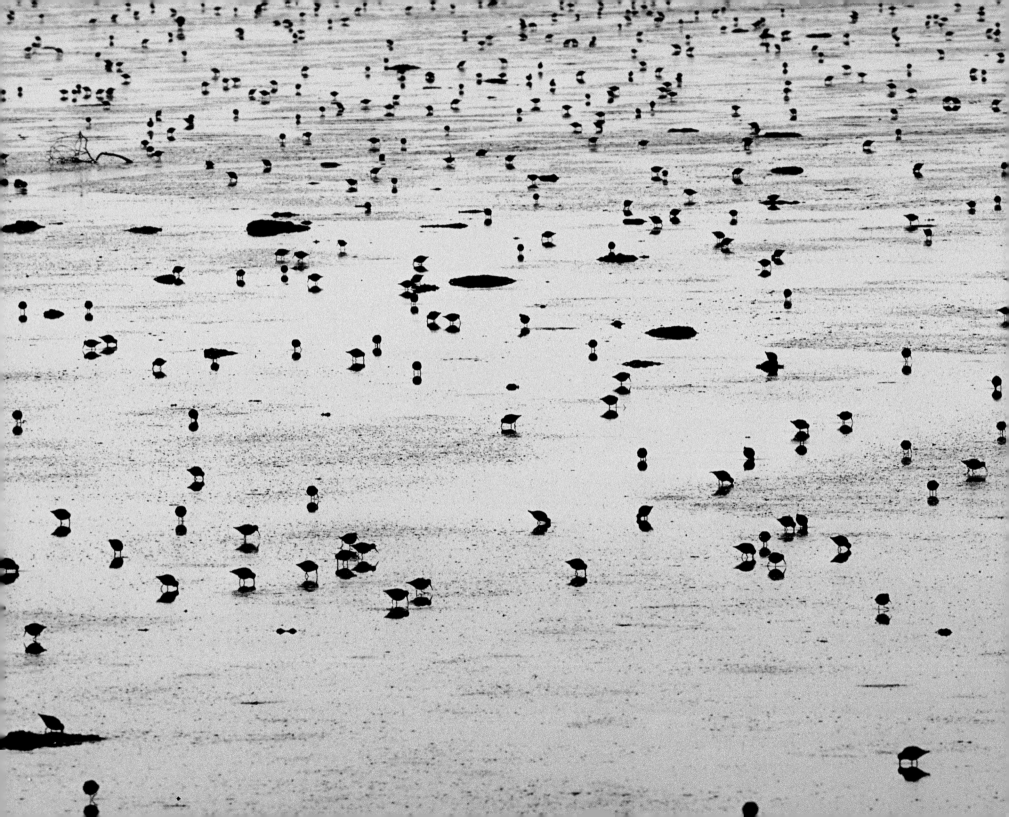

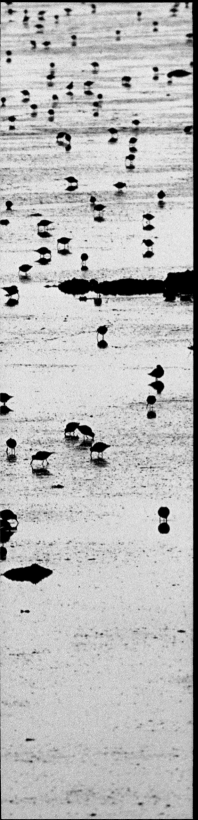

Located along the Delaware Bay in northeastern Delaware, Bombay Hook National Wildlife Refuge is renowned for its spectacular concentrations of migrating waterfowl. More than 100,000 greater snow geese and 50,000 ducks of various species converge each fall and winter onto the refuge's wetlands and fields. Established in 1937, Bombay Hook protects 12,000 acres of salt marsh, one of the largest untouched marshes along the entire east coast. Because of its location along the Atlantic Flyway, the refuge is a critical migratory bird stopover. Here waterfowl, shorebirds, and songbirds can rest and refuel before disembarking on their journey to more favorable southern climates.

With its extensive expanses of salt marshes and exposed mud flats, the refuge also plays hosts to thousands of migrating shorebirds during the spring and fall migration seasons. Bombay is one of the nation's top locations for shorebird watching.

One cool, crisp autumn morning at the refuge, I saw the sun reflecting its gold brilliance on an exposed tidal flat and just like magic, a flock of semipalmated sandpipers suddenly landed. I used a telephoto lens to isolate portions of the scene, emphasizing the shorebird silhouettes against a backdrop of solid solar gold.

Overleaf: Oyster shells, Eastern Neck National Wildlife Refuge, Maryland.

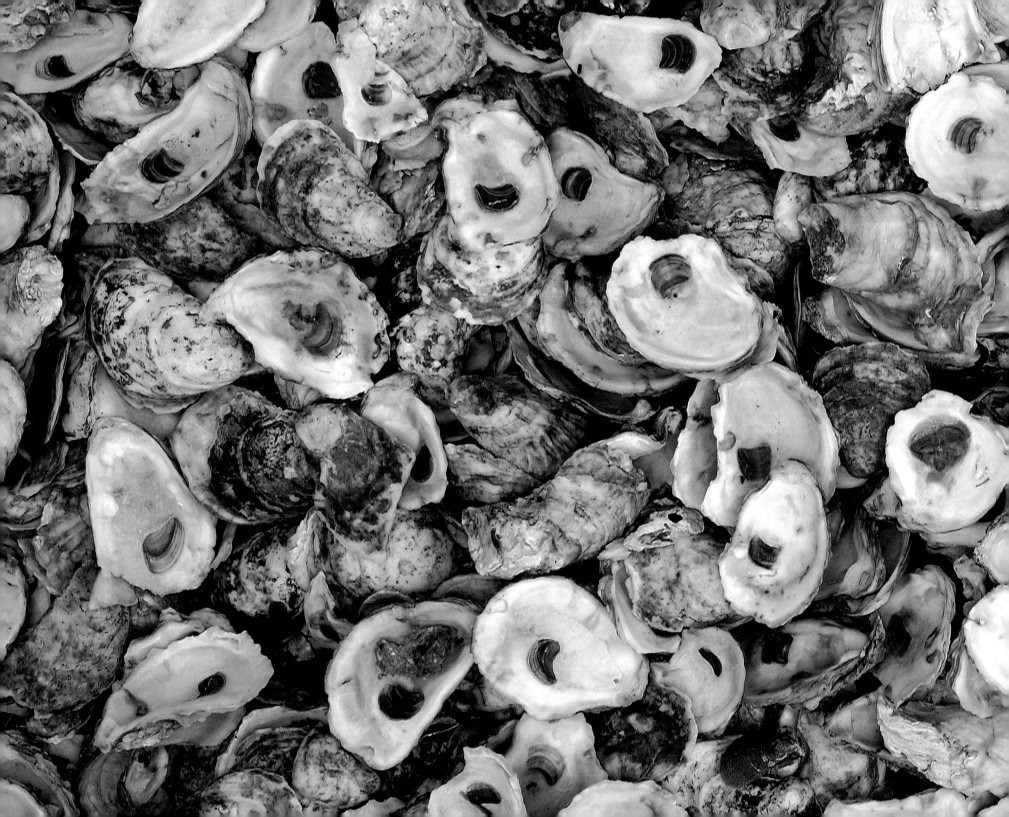

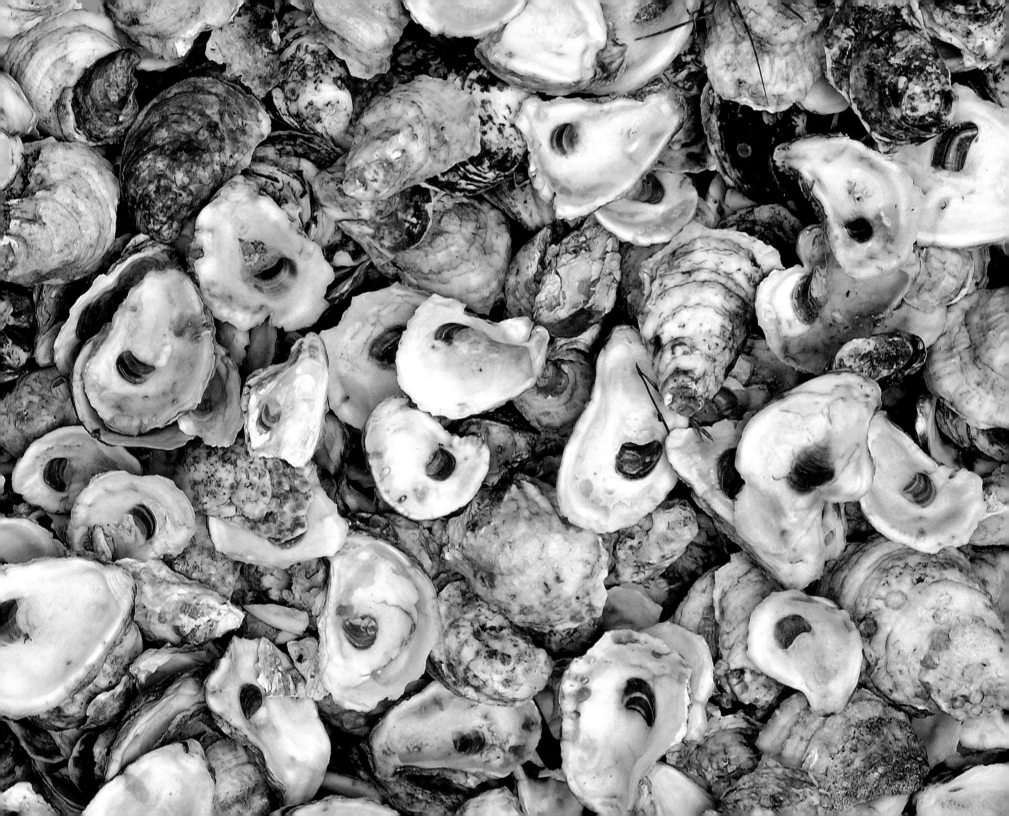

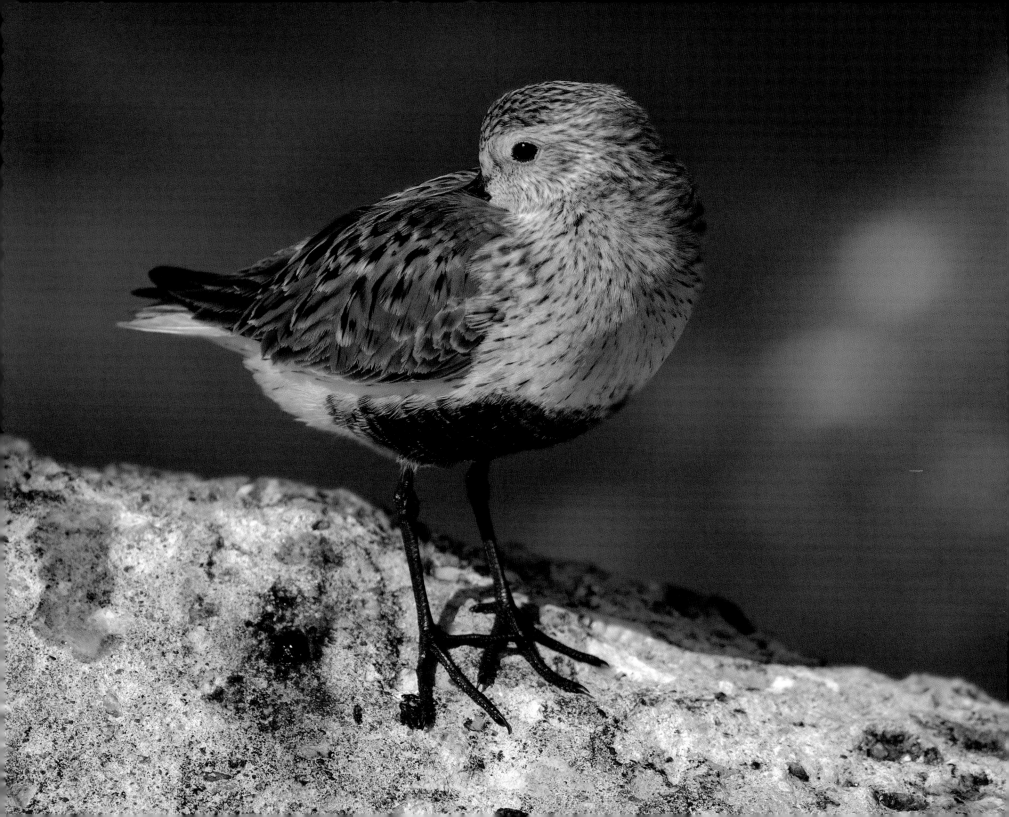

The last nine miles of the narrow road leading to Elliot Island passes through an amazing stretch of vast salt marsh, referred to locally as "Maryland's Everglades." Hammocks of loblolly pine dot the landscape, providing important habitat for nesting songbirds and the bald eagle. Bordered by the Nanticoke River on the west and Fishing Bay to the east, Elliot Island lies within the 21,000 acre Fishing Bay Wildlife Management Area. This state managed landscape protects nesting and wintering habitat for a variety of wetland and marsh birds, including ospreys, harriers, and several species of rails, herons, and egrets. The salt marsh provides important nursery grounds for crabs and fish.

At the end of the road is a small boat dock and landing. Bordering the shoreline are blocks of concrete rip-rap, and it is here where I captured this close-up image of a dunlin in its colorful breeding plumage. As part of a larger flock of maybe 200 – 300 dunlins, this particular dunlin was resting on top of the rip-rap. I got down to their eye-level and slowly made my way to the resting flock. With a strong spring wind whipping around me, the birds were reluctant to take flight. Using my 600mm telephoto lens along with a 1.4 tele-converter, I was able to get full-frame images without getting too close to these beautiful shorebirds. Along with the dunlins were hundreds of ruddy turnstones and short-billed dowitchers, all resting before taking flight to their arctic breeding grounds.

Overleaf: Semi-palmated plover, Chincoteague National Wildlife Refuge, Virginia.

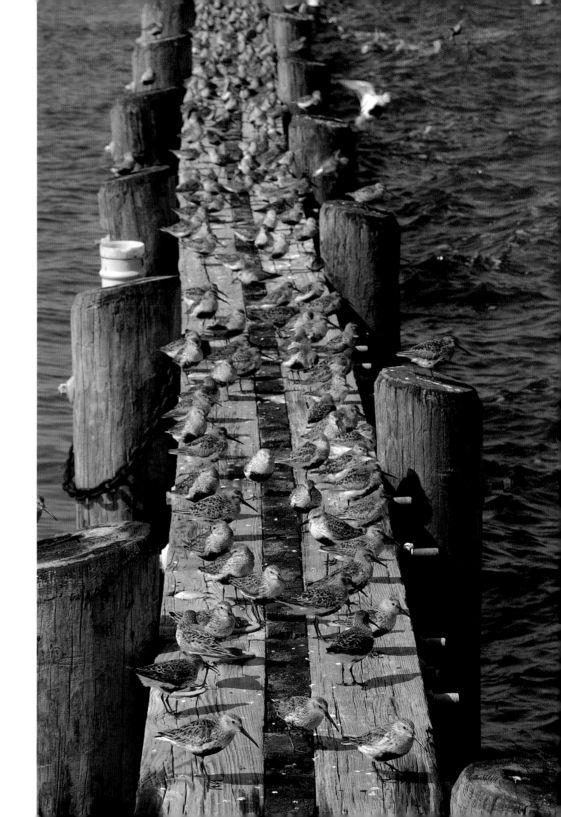

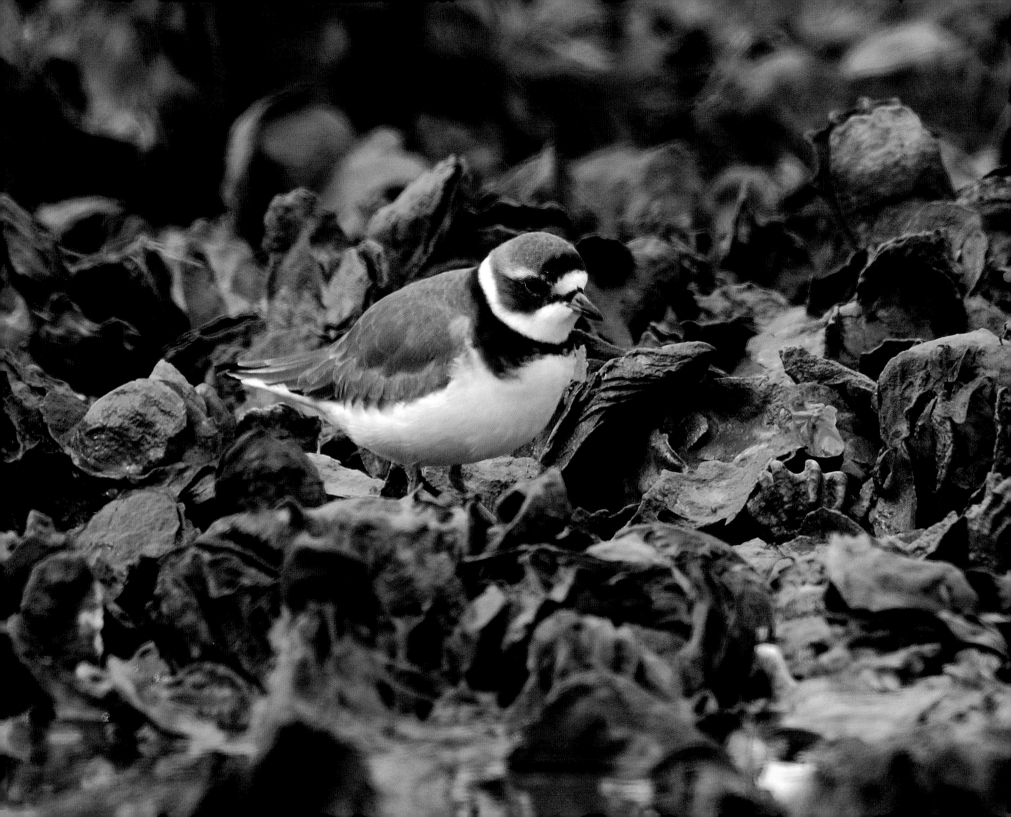

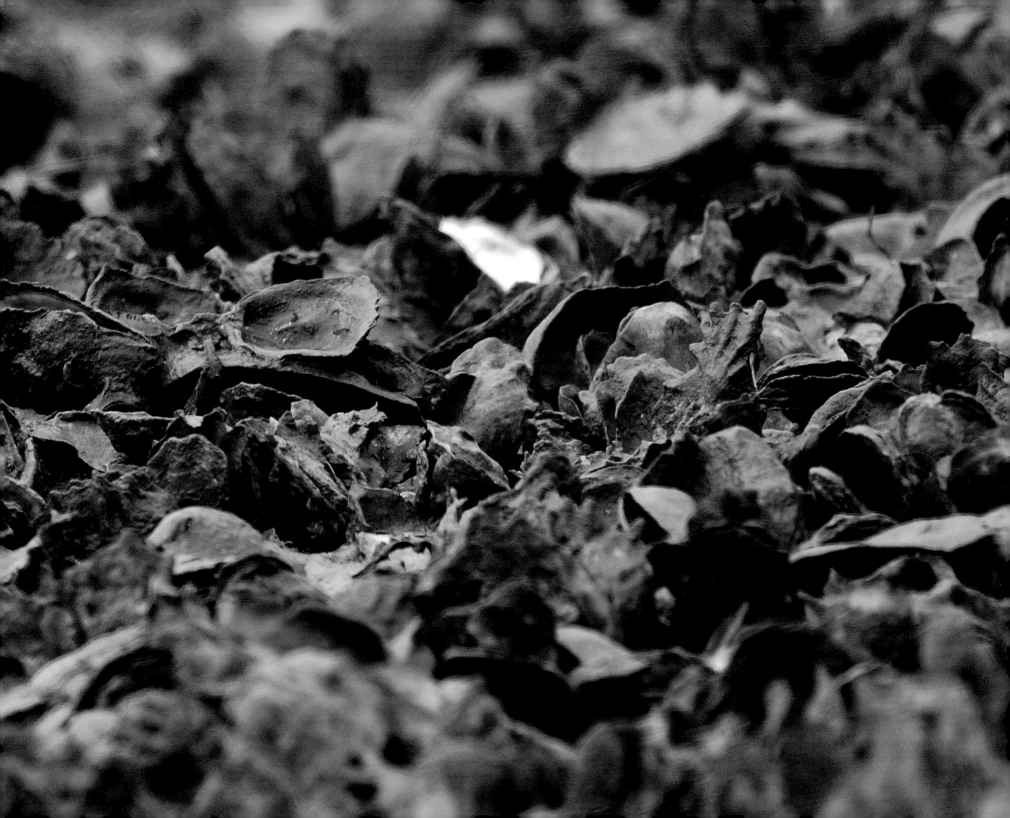

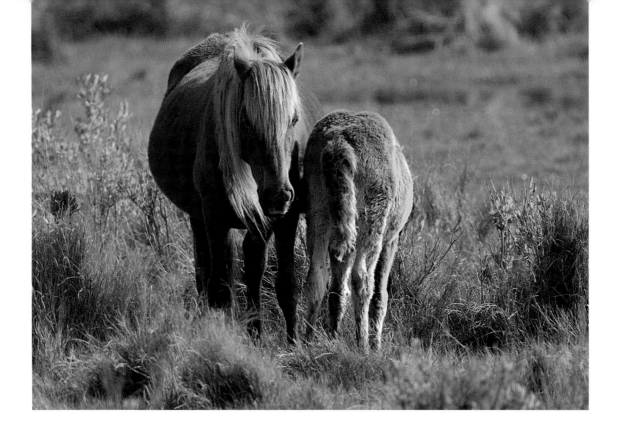

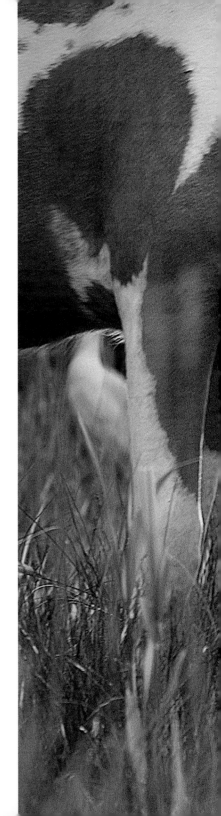

The wild ponies of Chincoteague are steeped in legend. The romantic version of how the ponies arrived stems from the tale of a ship-wrecked Spanish galleon in the 1600s. The horses swam ashore and adapted to an extreme environment of sand, salt, mosquitoes, and stifling summer temperatures. The most likely story, however, has to do with local settlers moving their livestock to the island to avoid paying taxes. Regardless of which story folks believe, the horses are here and have been an integral part of the island's history. While a major attraction for tourists to the refuge, the horses remain controversial in terms of their affect on native flora and fauna.

The horses are not native to the island and thus, over time have created management challenges to the refuge. The horses are now located on two fenced compartments on the refuge to prevent the herd from adversely affecting the sensitive barrier island vegetation. The Virginia herd is owned and managed by the Chincoteague Volunteer Fire Department. An annual pony roundup, which occurs every July, draws thousands of folks to the island as "saltwater cowboys" herd the horses across the Assateague Channel to the island of Chincoteague. From there some of the foals and yearlings are auctioned to the highest bidder. The revenue generated from the sales of the ponies goes back to the Chincoteague Fire Department. The annual pony penning and auction also helps to keep the herd at a manageable population of around 150.

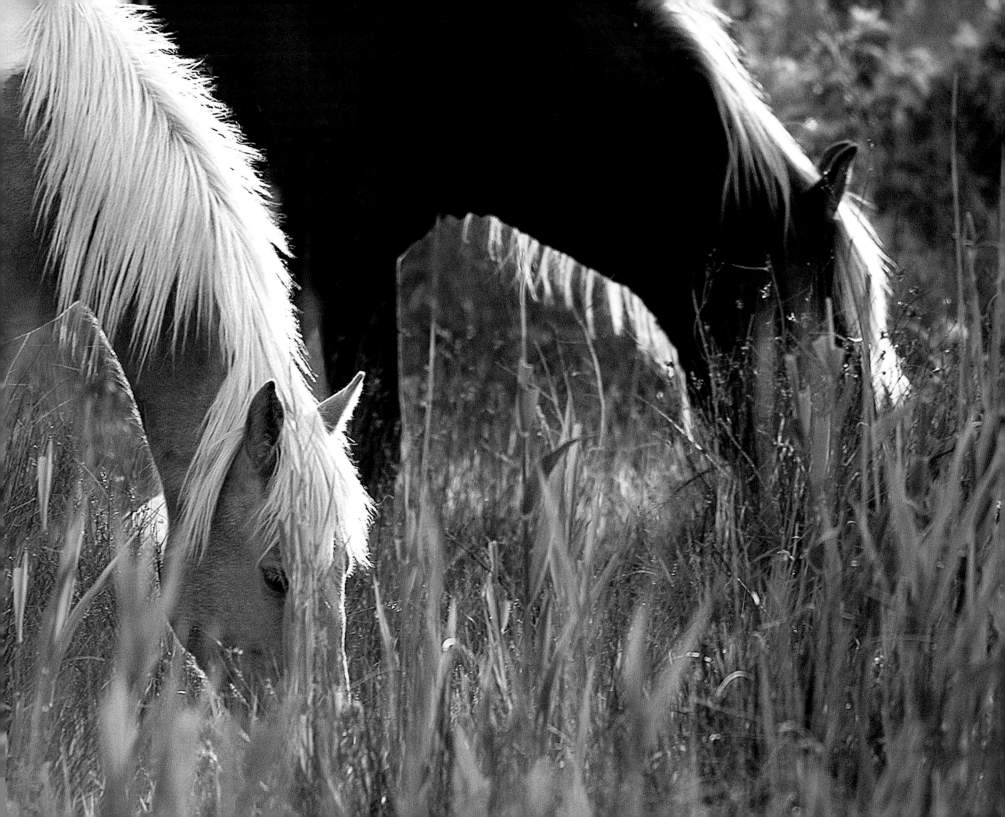

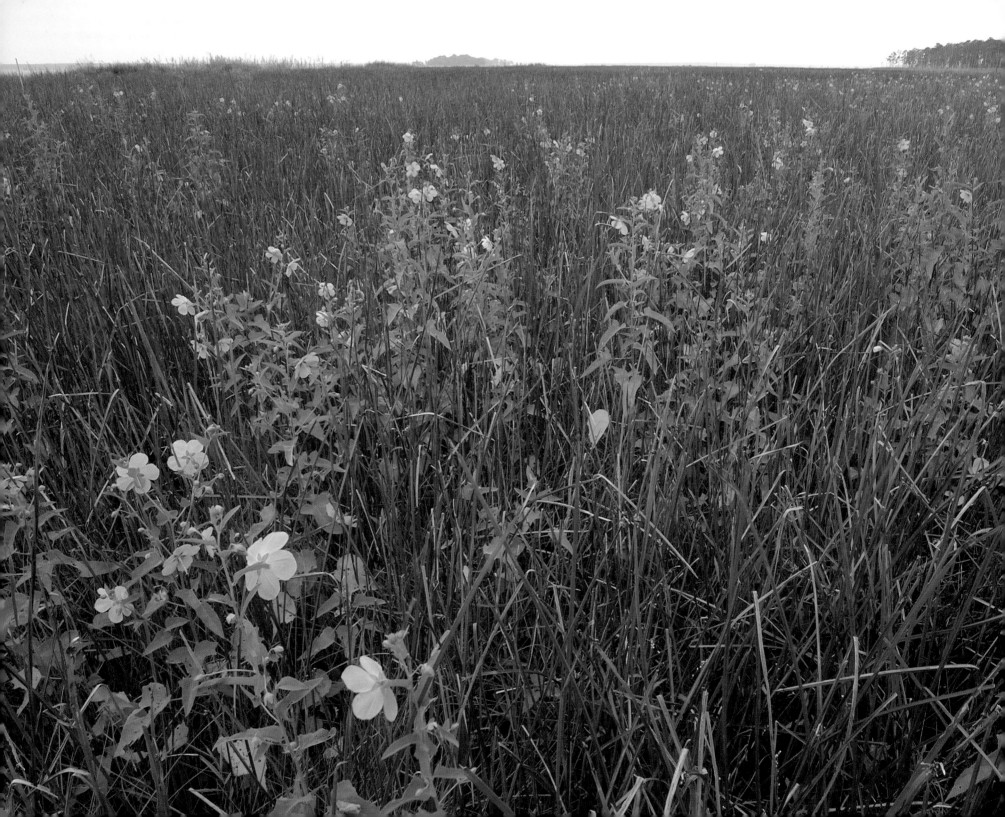

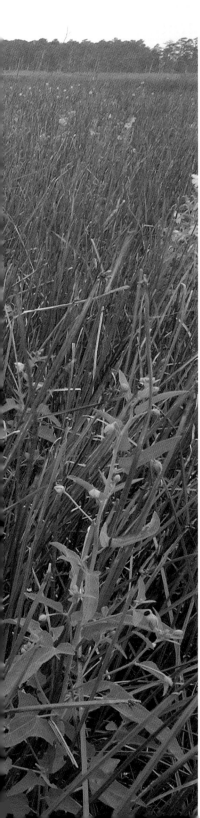

The emerald-green expanse of wind-swept tidal marshes along the Eastern Shore is one of the most productive ecosystems in the world. Rich in species diversity – both plant and animal – the landscape appears rather simple in structure. But a closer look reveals a complex arrangement of water, life, and process, each working in synch to produce a world of extraordinary abundance and composition. Fed by hundreds of rivers and creeks and the continual movement of the tides, the brackish waters of the Chesapeake Bay alone harbors more than 2,500 species of animals and plants.

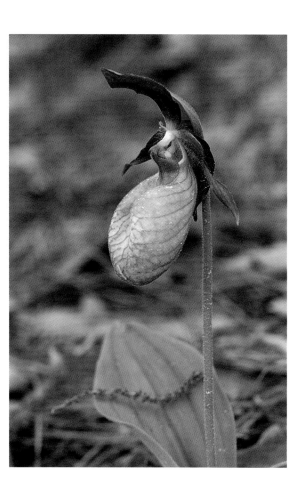

This image of the tidal marshes of Blackwater National Wildlife Refuge was captured one July afternoon. The temperatures were rather mild for the middle of summer and the humidity hanging in the air was almost non-existent. Very few biting insects were attacking me. An afternoon thunderstorm was gathering strength to the west, but was still several miles from where I was photographing.

While I was photographing, a couple of bald eagles flew overhead. Marsh wrens sang from the safety of the marsh. Patches of yellow bladderwort protruding just above the water's surface provided a colorful addition to the black-stained water. Pink marsh mallows dotted the green landscape. Dragonflies with names like meadowhawk, darner, and shadow dragon dashed back and forth over the marsh, while a single red-winged blackbird perched nearby, singing loudly – obviously taking exception to my intrusion into his territory.

Above: Pink lady's slipper, Chincoteague National Wildlife Refuge, Virginia.

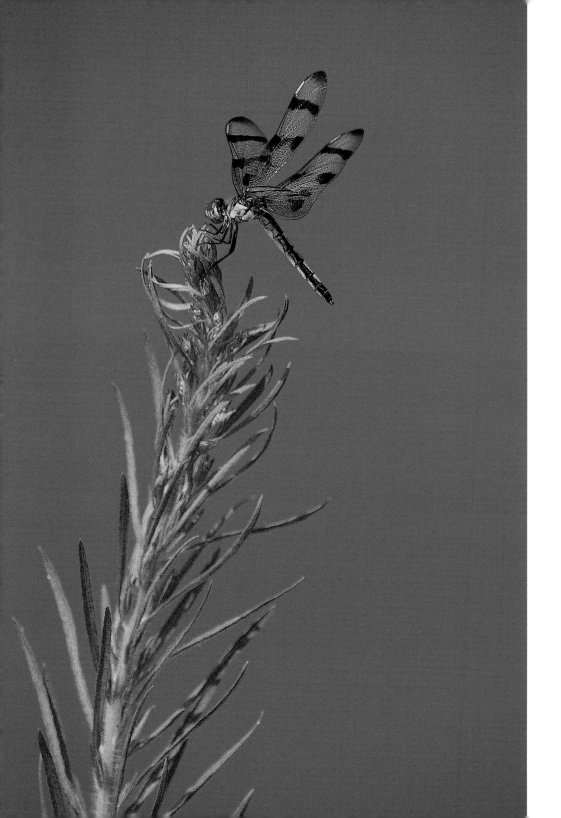

More than 300 of the 3,000 species of dragonflies in the world are found in North America, and there is no better place to watch dragonflies than along the wetlands and meadows of the Eastern Shore. From summer to early autumn, these aerial acrobats appear in the thousands over every available open body of water. While these insects can be a bit intimidating to humans, I find solace in that they are doing a great job consuming a ton of mosquitoes that might otherwise be attacking me.

While driving along the auto tour route at Blackwater National Wildlife Refuge one hot July day, I decided to try my luck photographing the dragonflies diving and darting over the marsh. Although it was mid-day and the sun was relentless in its intensity, I started hiking down the tour route. Using a 600mm telephoto lens and aided by the increased focal length factor of a digital camera, I was able to stay a considerable distance away from the dragonflies.

With the direct lighting from the sun and a clean background, I was able to capture images of the dragonflies as they perched on the stems of marsh grass bordering the wetland. It is moments like these when nature photographers forget about the challenges 90 degree temperatures and high humidity exerts on the human body. We become lost in the wonders of nature that surround us and we remain steadfast in capturing these moments on film and flash card.

More than 60 species of butterflies occur along the Eastern Shore and with the ever-growing popularity of "butterfly watching," the coastal habitats of Delaware, Maryland, and Virginia are prime locations for nature enthusiasts to see these flying colors of life. National wildlife refuges such as Blackwater and Eastern Neck have excellent butterfly gardens that attract hundreds of butterflies. Efforts to encourage native species of wildflowers at national wildlife refuges and along roadsides and in abandoned meadows are also enhancing habitats for butterflies. The native cardinal flower is one of the most preferred nectar sources for butterflies.

This spicebush swallowtail butterfly was photographed during one sultry July afternoon at the butterfly garden at Eastern Neck National Wildlife Refuge. Many of the hundreds of butterflies floating around me were a bit ragged in appearance, so some effort was required to find a subject that wasn't too beat up. Most butterfly photography involves using a flash and hand holding the camera, but with strong lighting and having no where else to go for the afternoon, I decided to place my camera on a tripod, use patience, and rely on the natural light to capture this image. The butterflies were rather oblivious to me as I slowly roamed from one flower to the next before photographing this spicebush swallowtail on a very tall and prime cardinal flower.

Overleaf: Tiger swallowtails can be seen at many of the Eastern Shore's natural areas, particularly Eastern Shore of Virginia National Wildlife Refuge, located at the southern tip of the Delmarva Peninsula.

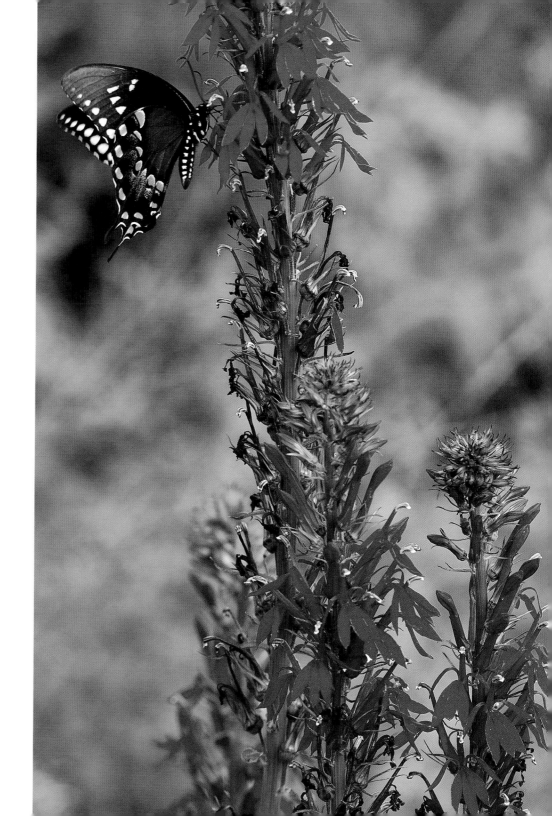

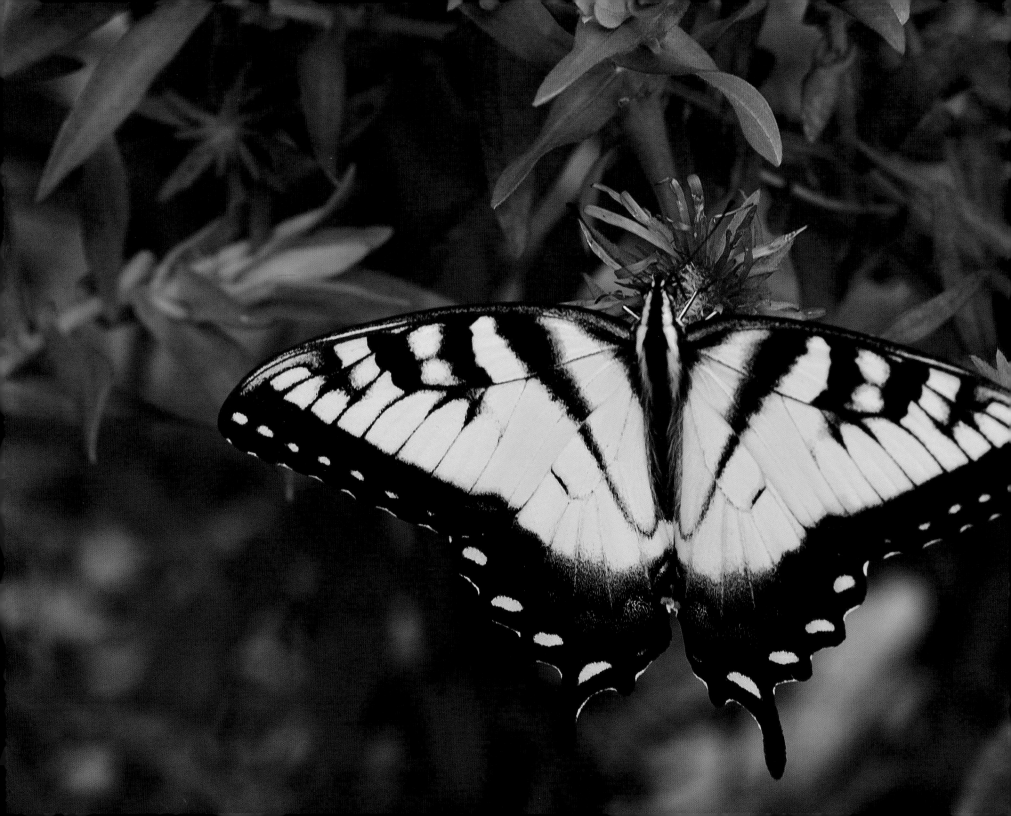

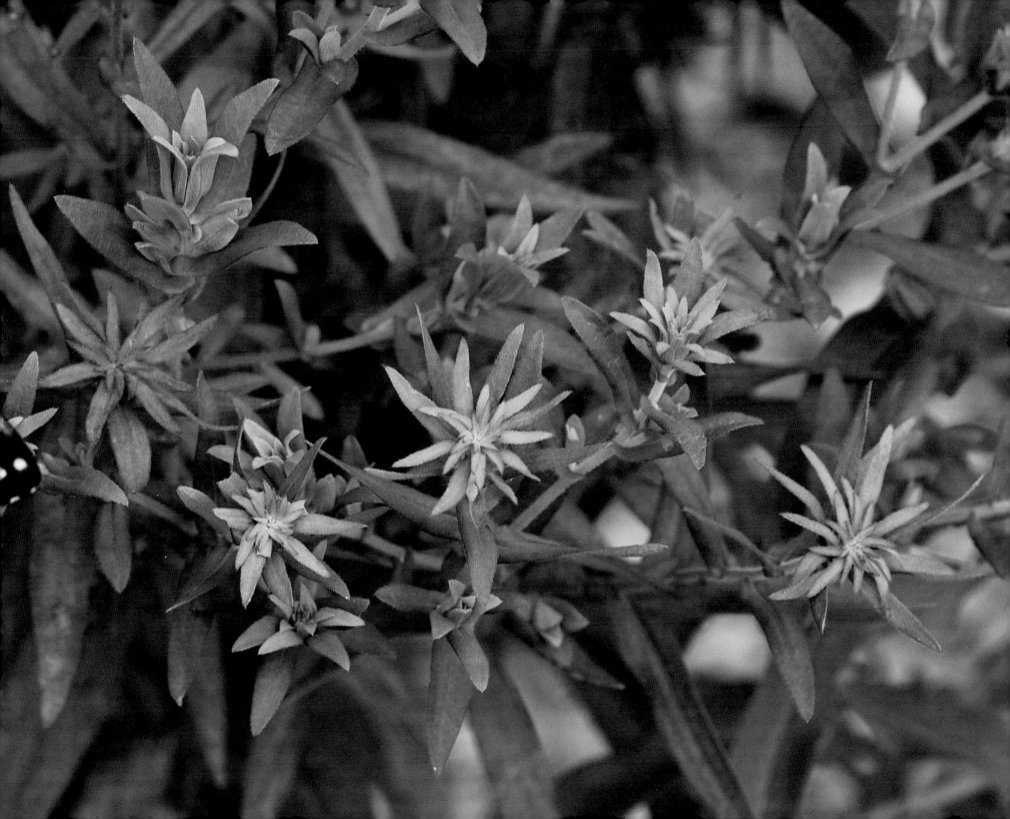

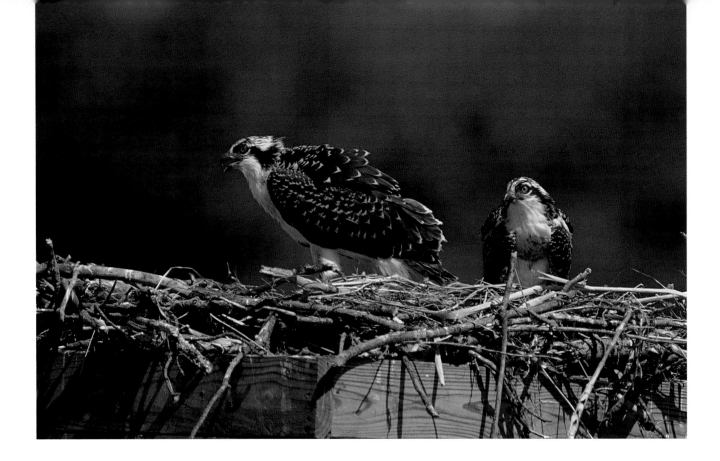

The osprey – also known as the fish hawk – is a story of success along the Eastern Shore. During the 1950s and 60s the osprey, as well as other fish-eating birds such as the bald eagle and brown pelican, experienced serious declines in their populations; victims all of the unrestricted use of pesticides, especially DDT. Ingesting pesticide-contaminated fish, the female birds laid eggs that were thin-shelled, enough to easily crack when the adults tried to incubate them on the nest.

In 1962 the book *Silent Spring* by Rachel Carson brought attention to the world about the dangers of these pesticides and the effects to our nation's birdlife. Thankfully, the public and politicians paid heed to this environmental disaster. Quick action was taken to restrict or ban the use of these pesticides. Ospreys have significantly rebounded to the point that these beautiful creatures are an everyday sight along the Eastern Shore during the spring and summer months.

While exploring the road leading to Elliot Island one early summer morning, I decided to photograph a pair of young ospreys on a nesting platform near the boat landing at the end of the road. Using my 600mm telephoto, I slowly walked along the edge of the shoreline to capture this simple composition of the birds complimented by a beautiful blue summer sky.

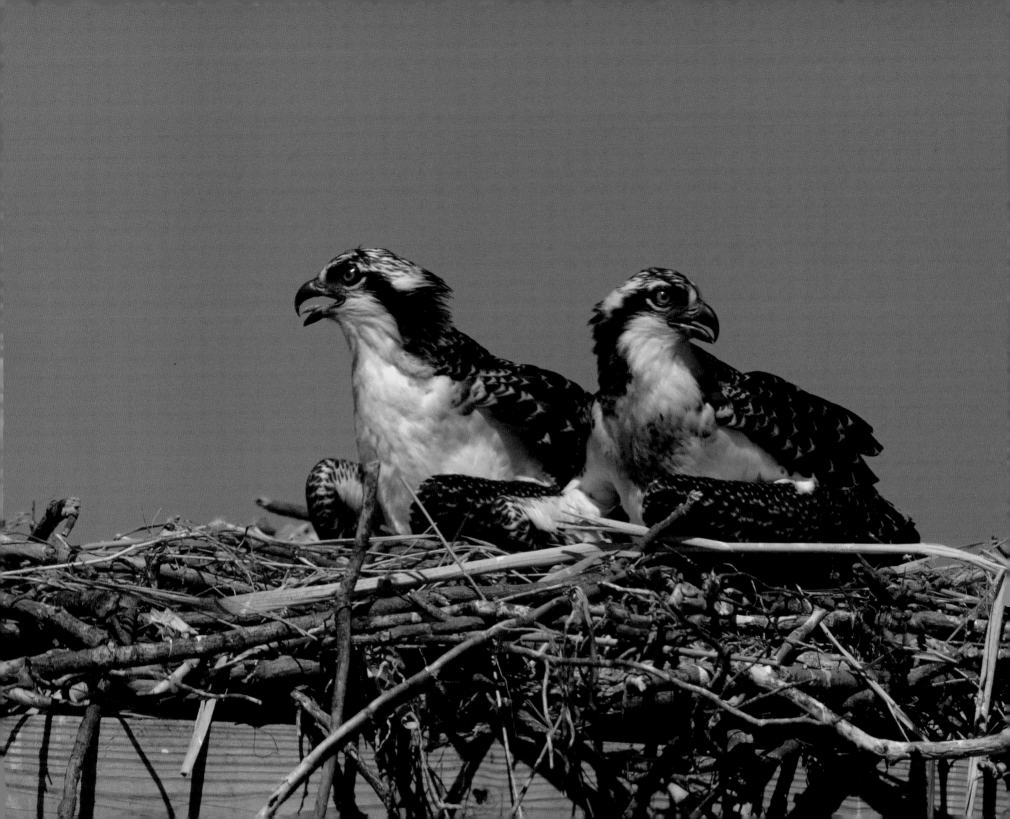

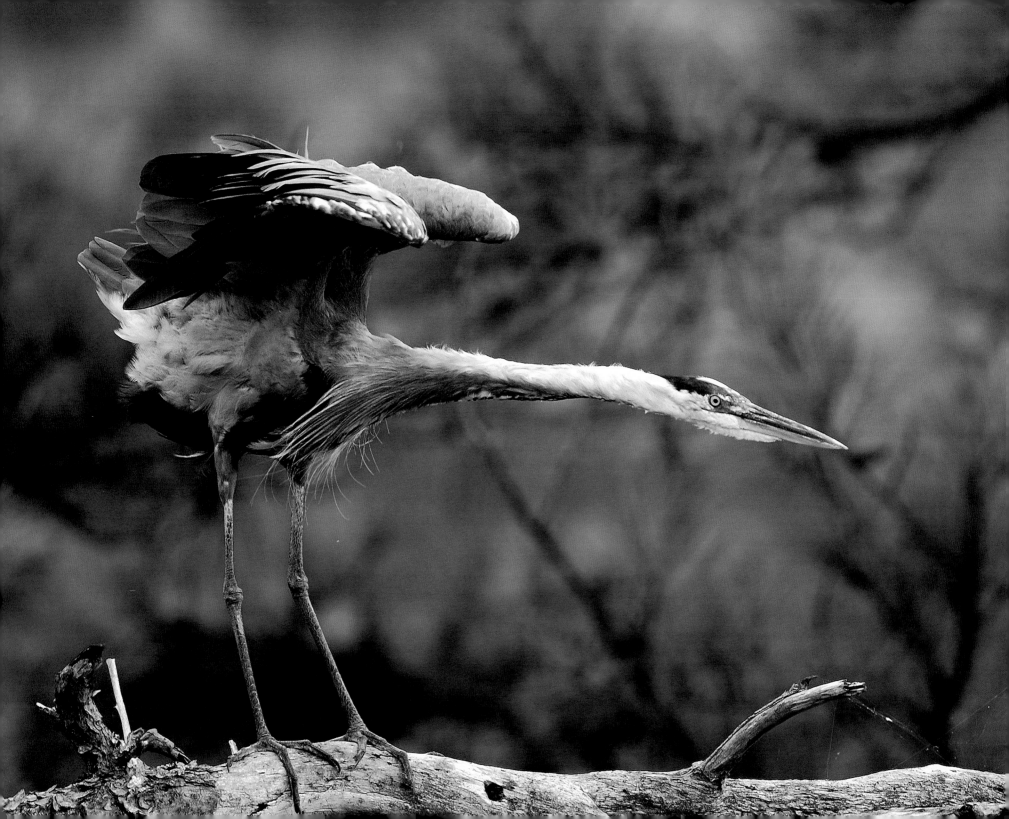

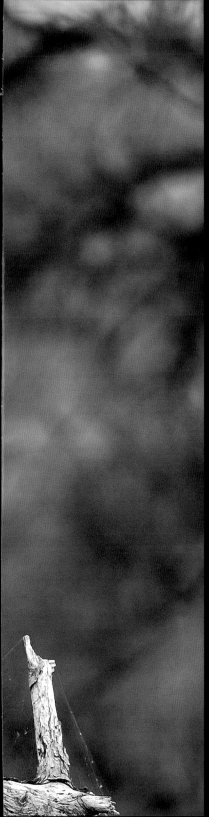

Sometimes nature photographers get so wrapped up in the moment, they forget to stop, look, and listen. This image is an example of making sure to look up from your viewfinder once in awhile to see what else might be worth photographing nearby.

This image was captured during a sultry mid-summer morning at Blackwater National Wildlife Refuge. Temperatures hovered in the low 90s, but the humidity was extraordinarily low for this time of the year, making this morning on the marsh more tolerable than usual.

My attention was focused on photographing images of the refuge's vast marsh landscape. At one point I looked up from my viewfinder and saw a lone great blue heron fly over and land on a loblolly pine. I decided to try my luck at photographing it.

The heron was in no hurry to leave and I wasn't in a rush to do anything else either. So for a considerable length of time I photographed the heron as it rested, preened, and stretched from its lofty perch above the marsh. In nature photography, it is often the unsuspected moments captured on film or flash card that brings the most joy to the photographer.

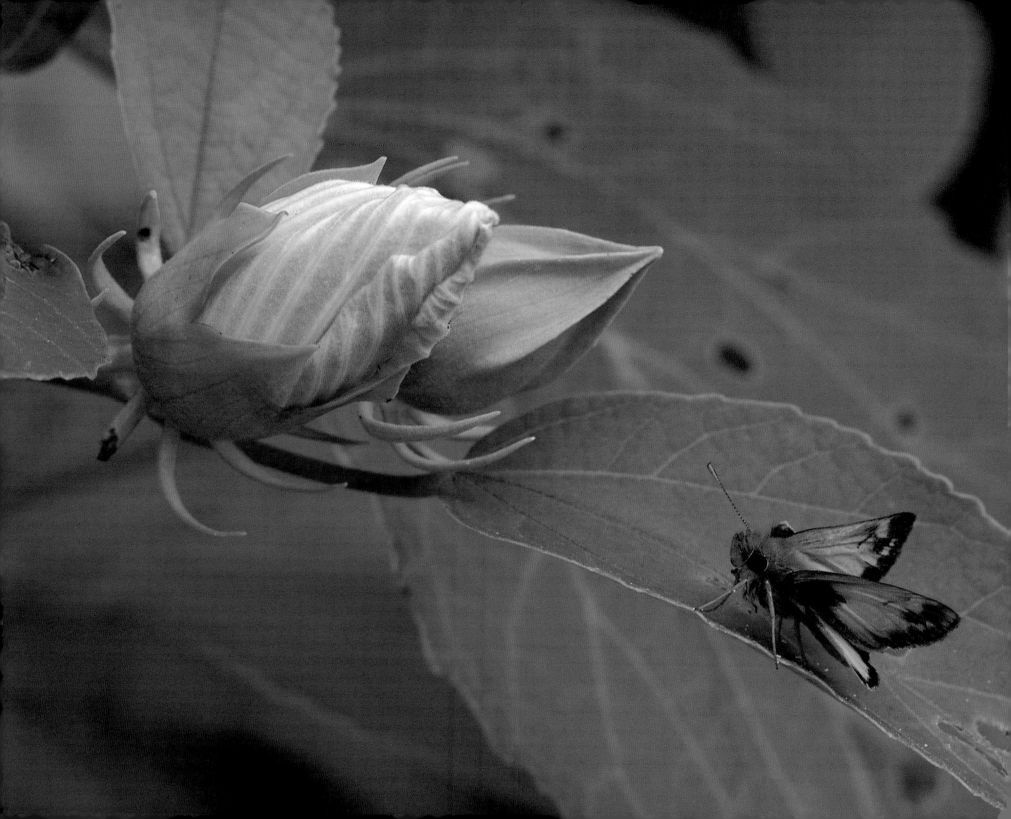

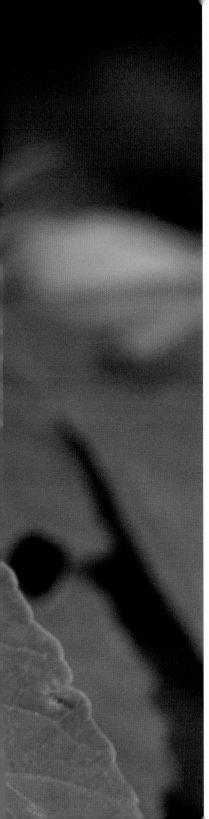

More than 3,500 species of skippers occur worldwide. The Eastern Shore is home to 85 of these small and often ignored insects. Skippers get their name from their rapid and erratic flight behavior. Not considered true butterflies since their bodies are proportionately larger than their wings, skippers present a challenge to the butterfly enthusiasts. Close and careful examination of them is required to get a decent identification. Additionally, true to their names, skippers do a lot of "skipping," flying quickly from one flower to the next. Any slight movement can sometimes set them off on another erratic flight.

While photographing a cluster of marsh hibiscus one hot and humid August afternoon at Eastern Neck National Wildlife Refuge near Rock Hall, Maryland, I noticed several skippers flying from one flower to the next. This particular skipper landed right next to the flower I was photographing. I was afforded several minutes of photography time before it decided to move on. Passing clouds acted as giant diffusers to help eliminate the harsh light from the mid-day summer sun.

Photographing butterflies requires a bit of personal perseverance and patience. For photographers that can hold still for several minutes, the butterflies sometimes become accustomed to their presence.

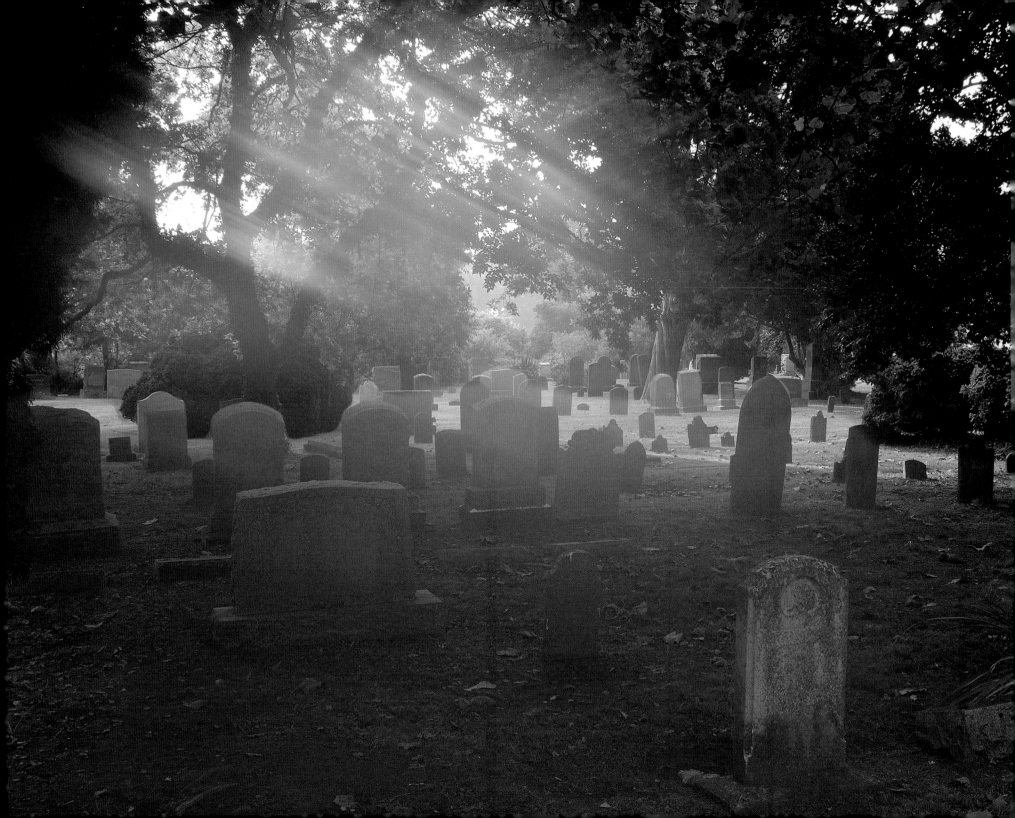

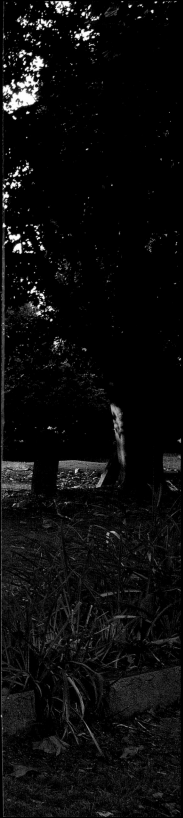

The community of Church Creek in Dorchester County took its name from the Old Trinity Church located a few miles to the west on Highway 16. Old Trinity was built around 1675 and remains active to this day, making it the oldest active Episcopal Church in the country.

The cemetery on the church grounds is steeped in history, with revolutionary war veterans, state governors, and Anna Eila Carroll, the "unofficial member of Lincoln's cabinet," buried here. A walk through the church grounds gives one a deep sense of the cultural and historical significance that Dorchester County played in the formation of the country.

To the east on Greenbrier Road near Blackwater National Wildlife Refuge is another site of national historical importance: the birthplace of Harriet Tubman, the famous Underground Railroad leader. Although Tubman was successful in escaping slavery by fleeing to Philadelphia in 1849, she was determined to help others escape. For the next ten years Tubman risked her life to help bring more than 300 slaves to freedom. At one time there was even a bounty of $40,000 for her capture; dead or alive.

Dorchester County at one time was a thriving region built on harvesting natural resources from the land and water. While the seafood industry has experienced a drastic downturn, the county's agricultural industry still continues on steady course. Today, one of the major economic drivers for the county is tourism.

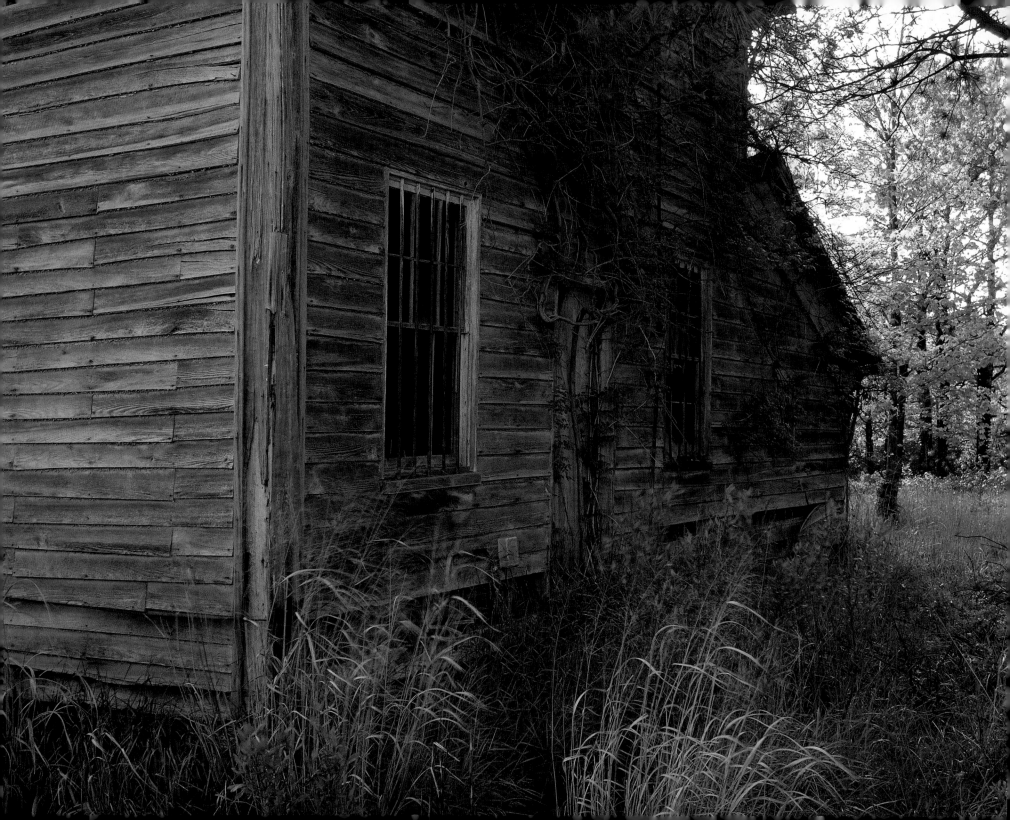

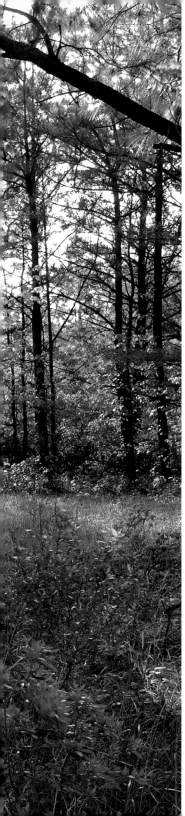

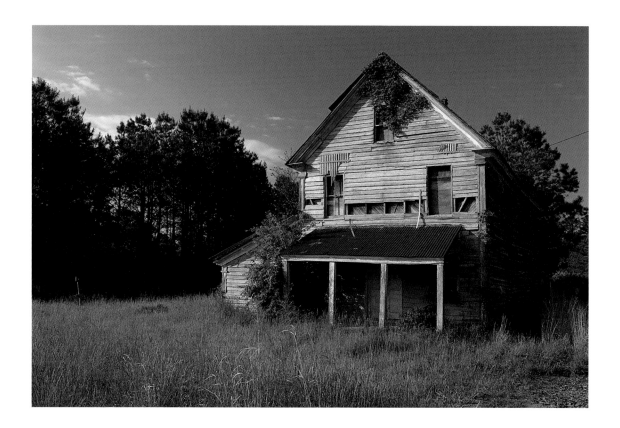

This old abandoned store is located at the intersection of Andrews Road and Shorters Wharf Road in the backcountry of Dorchester County. I'm not sure of the history of the building, but my imagination takes me to a time when the store was – outside the local churches – a gathering place for local residents to meet and socialize. The county's back roads are great places for discovering such icons of days gone by.

At one time Dorchester County had a substantial agricultural and fishing industry. The region's forestlands also sustained a thriving shipbuilding industry. With the exception of agriculture, the other land and water-based businesses have drastically declined over the years. I assume that many of these remote locations throughout the county had stores such as this one to service the families that lived and worked there. Today, they are just reminders of the region's rich history. And while many today yearn for a simpler quality of life, it's best to remember that in those days past, life wasn't any easier and in many situations, less convenient.

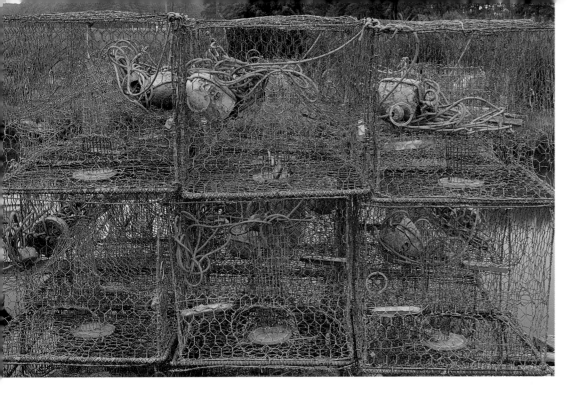

During an early morning drive from Cambridge to Taylor's Island, I saw this collection of colorful crab pots stacked near the highway. I was planning to photograph marsh scenes along the little Choptank River and Chesapeake Bay, but the weather was too windy and overcast for me to get the composition I had anticipated. I passed these crab pots a couple of times before stopping and taking the photograph. I was fascinated by the play of colors of the individual buoys within each pot.

This image is a constant reminder for me of a proud profession of waterman who ply the Bay waters in search of oysters in the winter and crabs during the summer. It's not an easy life, one that is becoming increasingly challenging with the dwindling stocks of fish, crabs, and oysters in the Chesapeake Bay and neighboring tributaries. The Bay is dying and the political ramifications of delayed funding to clean its waters are becoming critical in whether or not this once bountiful estuary will ever recover.

While many conservation efforts are underway to help reverse the decline of the Bay's water quality and natural resource values, it may be too little too late. Time will tell and we all hope the condition of the Chesapeake Bay will improve. Our nation's largest estuary ecosystem deserves better.

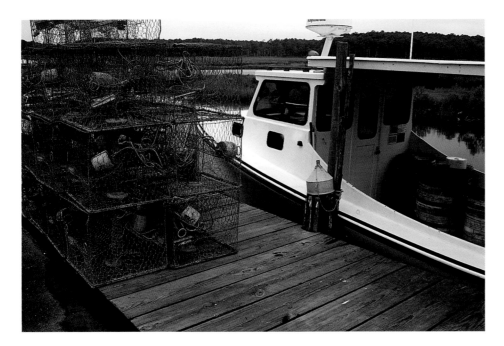

Left: Crab pots and boat, Hooper's Island, Maryland.

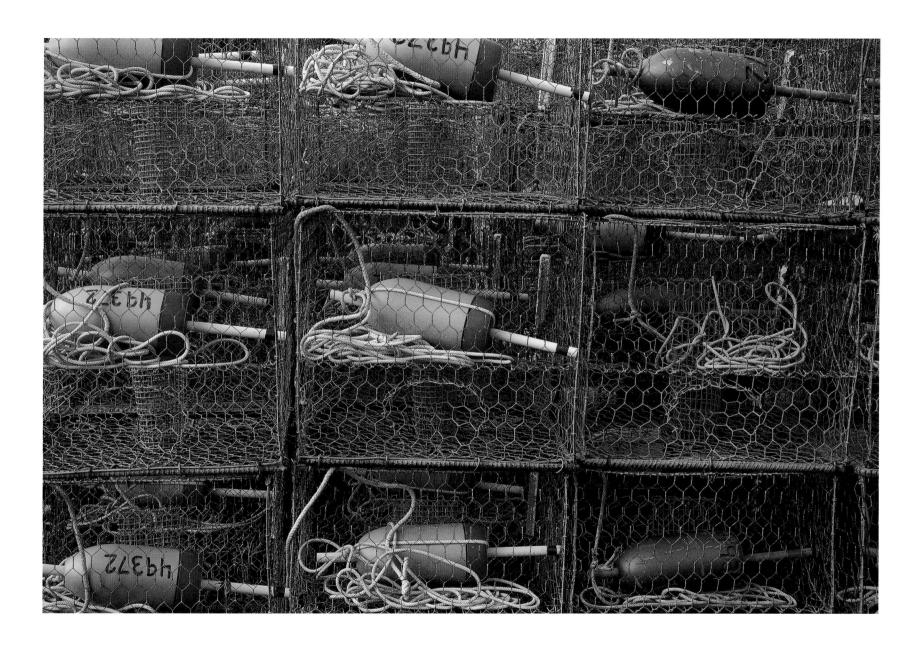

The southward migration of shorebirds along the Atlantic coast starts in earnest by mid-August. In early autumn, the tidal flats and marshes at Chincoteague become active with shorebirds. Fat reserves depleted, these weary long-distance migrants spend several days resting and feeding along the exposed tidal and mud flats on the refuge. Chincoteague at this time of the year serves as a vital refueling stop for thousands of shorebirds. After replenishing their energy reserves, the migrants depart for warmer climes in Central and South America.

The refuge actively manages 2,600 acres of freshwater impoundments to provide quality habitat for a variety of wildlife, including shorebirds. Water levels within these impoundments are lowered in late summer to early fall to coincide with the shorebird migration. Once the shorebirds have moved on, the water control structures in the impoundments are closed to allow rainwater to fill the impoundments to provide feeding sites for the next wave of migrants: migrating waterfowl.

While exploring the refuge's impoundments one early autumn afternoon, I saw a few marbled godwits among a flock of willets resting in Swans Cove. Although the willets are very common shorebirds to see at the refuge, the godwits are not as common and are always a welcomed treat for birders. In a driving rainstorm, I spent an afternoon photographing this particular godwit as it was preening among the sleeping willets.

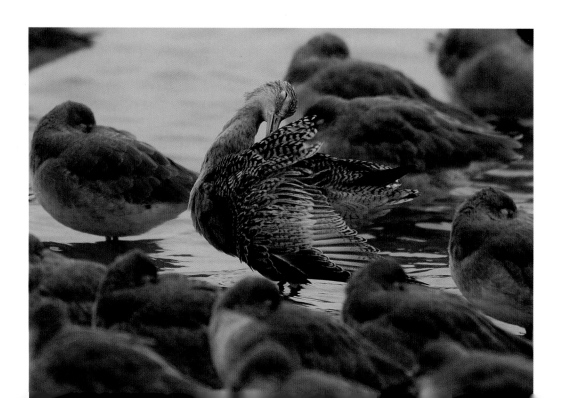

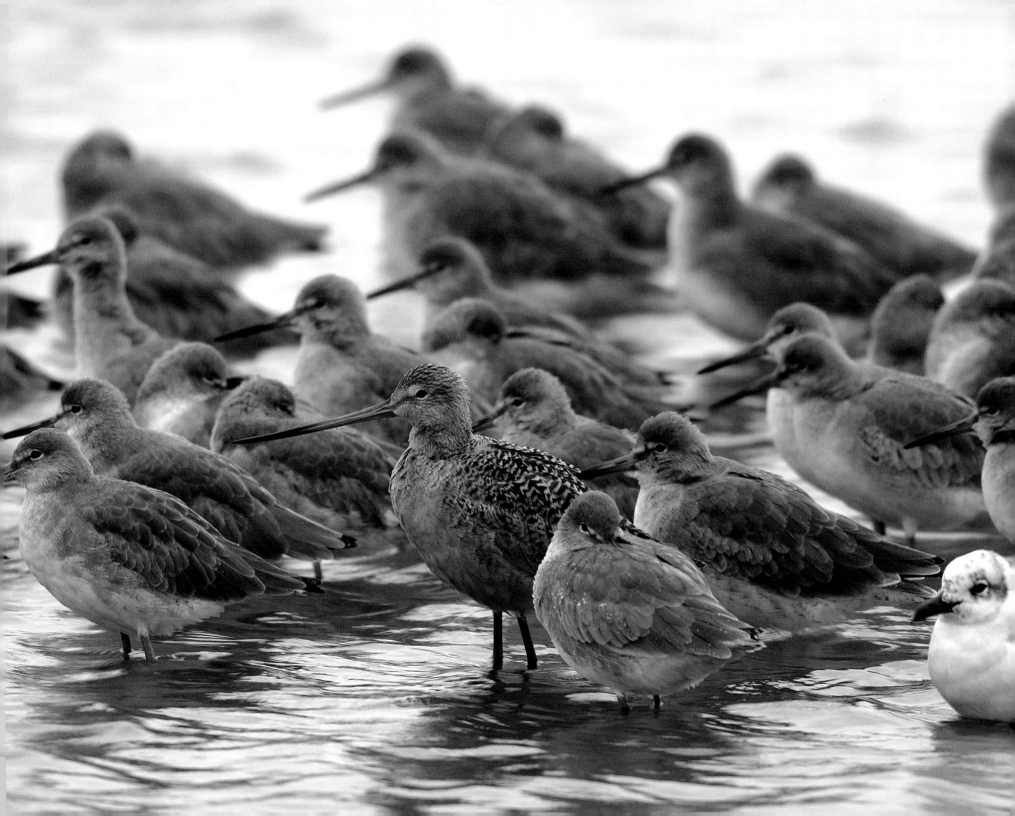

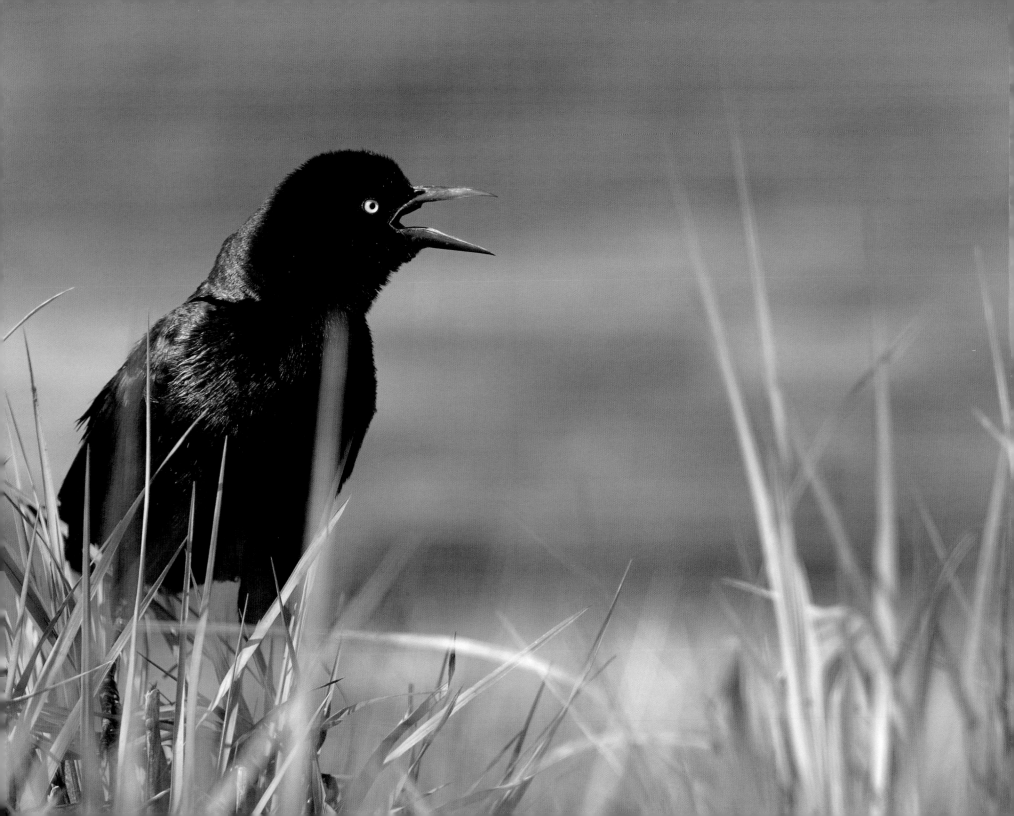

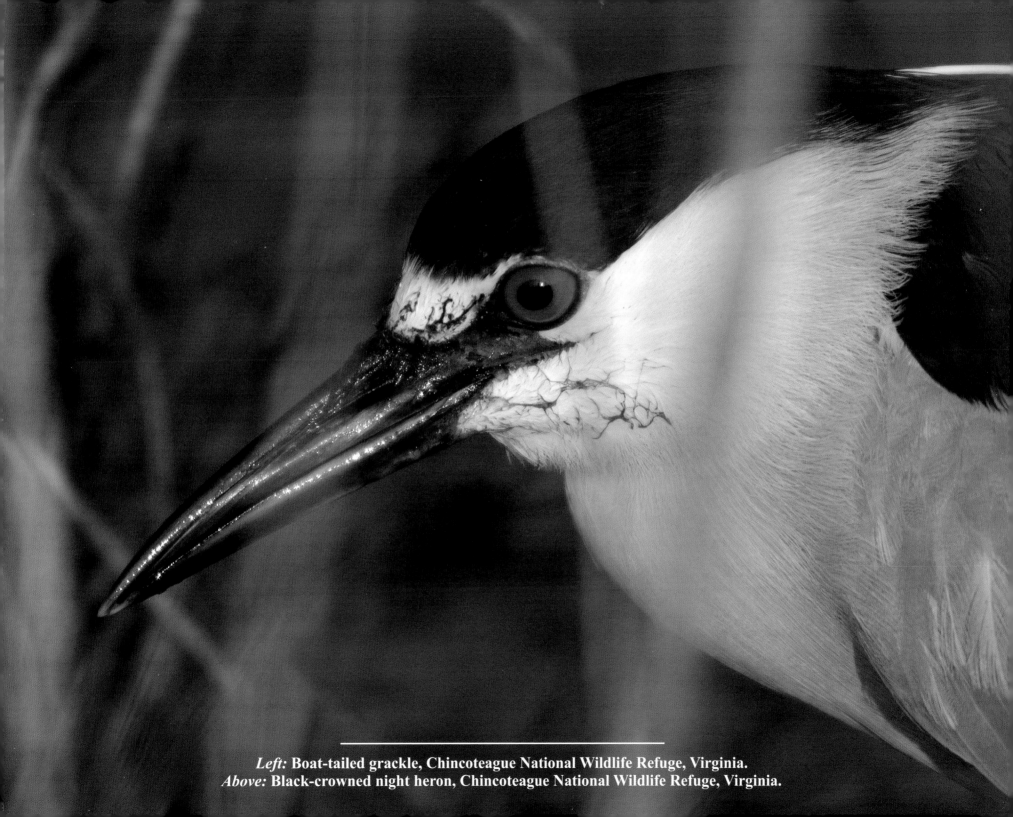

Left: **Boat-tailed grackle, Chincoteague National Wildlife Refuge, Virginia.**
Above: **Black-crowned night heron, Chincoteague National Wildlife Refuge, Virginia.**

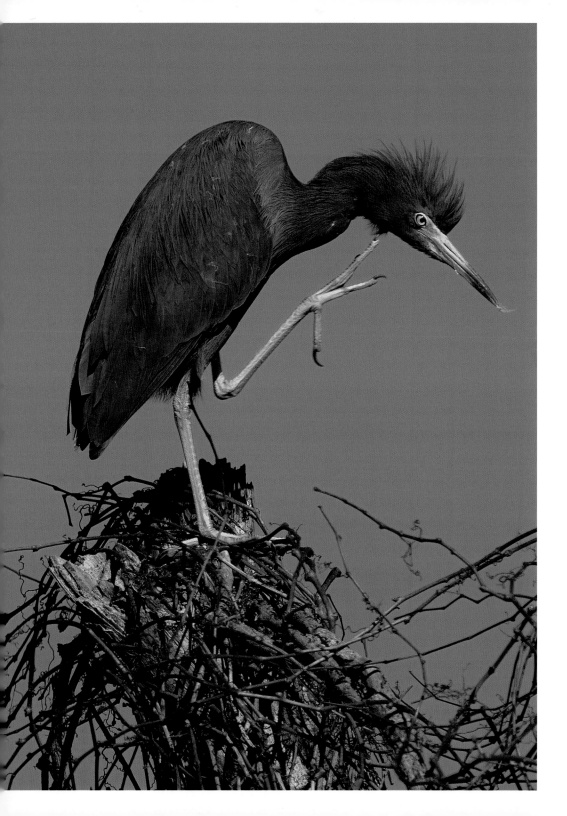

While not adorned with the showy filoplumes or aigrettes of its cousins the great egret and great blue heron, the little blue heron is nonetheless a most colorful and engaging member of the Eastern Shore's wading bird family.

Because of its habit of keeping its neck outstretched, the little blue seems to always be attentive or wary. But lest it be assumed the little blue is easy to approach, don't be fooled – it can be a formidable challenge to get up close and personal with this wading bird. But once in awhile, luck prevails and the bird lets down its guard.

This image was taken during one of those less guarded moments. The little blue had flown to the top of an old snag located on a small island near the terminus of Chincoteague's Wildlife Drive. Intent on preening and possibly soaking up the morning sun, the little blue paid no heed to the cars passing by or to one lone nature photographer (me).

With clear blue skies and the sun just above the horizon, the bird was in perfect light. When photographing birds, the best possible lighting to have is when the sun is directly behind you. This way, the subject becomes bathed in the golden rays of the sun. Of course, my 600mm telephoto lens with a 1.4x extender allowed me to get a nice portrait of the heron.

One early autumn morning while exploring Chincoteague National Wildlife Refuge, I was photographing a family of river otters as they were feeding and swimming along a borrow ditch beside Beach Road. Their persistent grunts and groans revealed their presence as they continued to swim along the ditch in search of fish and other aquatic life.

To get an opportunity to photograph them, I continually kept moving ahead of them, hoping for a clearing in the shrubby vegetation lining the ditch. At one location, I saw this immature black-crowned night heron perched beside the bank of the ditch. The heron was intently watching the water below, hoping to catch something for breakfast.

As the otters made their way to me, I noticed that the heron's attention was diverted to the otter's antics. The heron was more attracted to the otters than its original focus on getting something to eat. As the otters made their way past the inquisitive bird, the heron kept watching them until they had swam out of sight. I suppose even birds have an interest in natural entertainment.

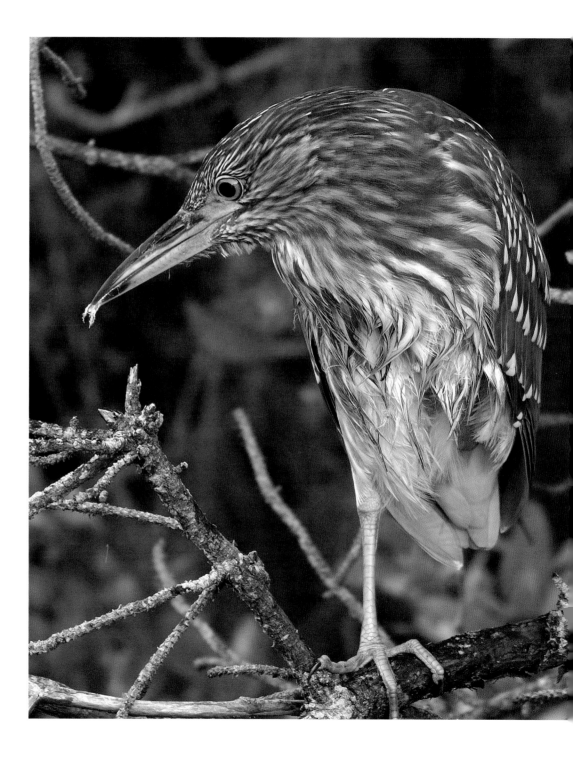

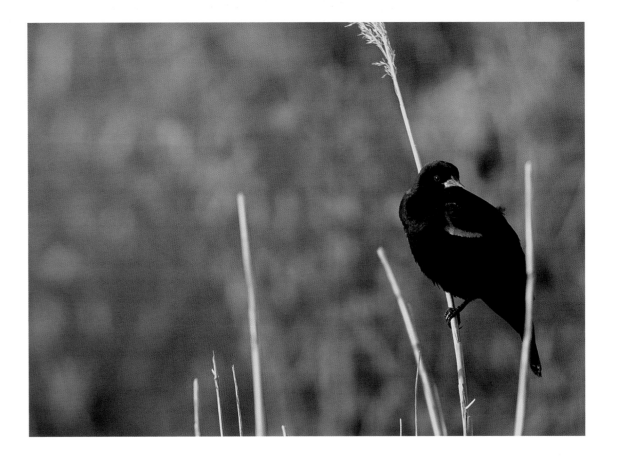

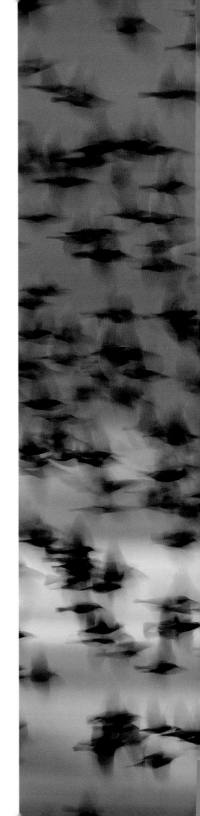

As with the great blue heron, the red-winged blackbird is an icon of the marshlands of the Eastern Shore. A glimpse of a male red-wing spreading its wings to show off its red epaulets is a sure sign of spring. There are not many birds in the marsh that can compete with such an elegantly plumed ebony body tinged with a bit of red and yellow on the shoulders. And to hear the red-wing's "konk-ka-ree" song is to know you are firmly implanted into a real sense of place for the Eastern Shore.

This image was taken along the wildlife tour route at Blackwater National Wildlife Refuge. Several flocks of red-wings were feeding in distant meadows, far from the reaches of even my most powerful telephoto lens. However, here's where a nature photographer practices patience and diligence ... and knowledge of animal behavior.

After several minutes of feeding on the ground, the flocks would explode into the sky and wing their way to another spot in the field. And each time they took flight, the flocks kept getting closer. Using my 600mm telephoto lens, I followed one particular flock. When the flock suddenly rose up and moved perpendicular to me, I snapped the shutter. You have to stay mindful and be quick to get these types of moments in nature.

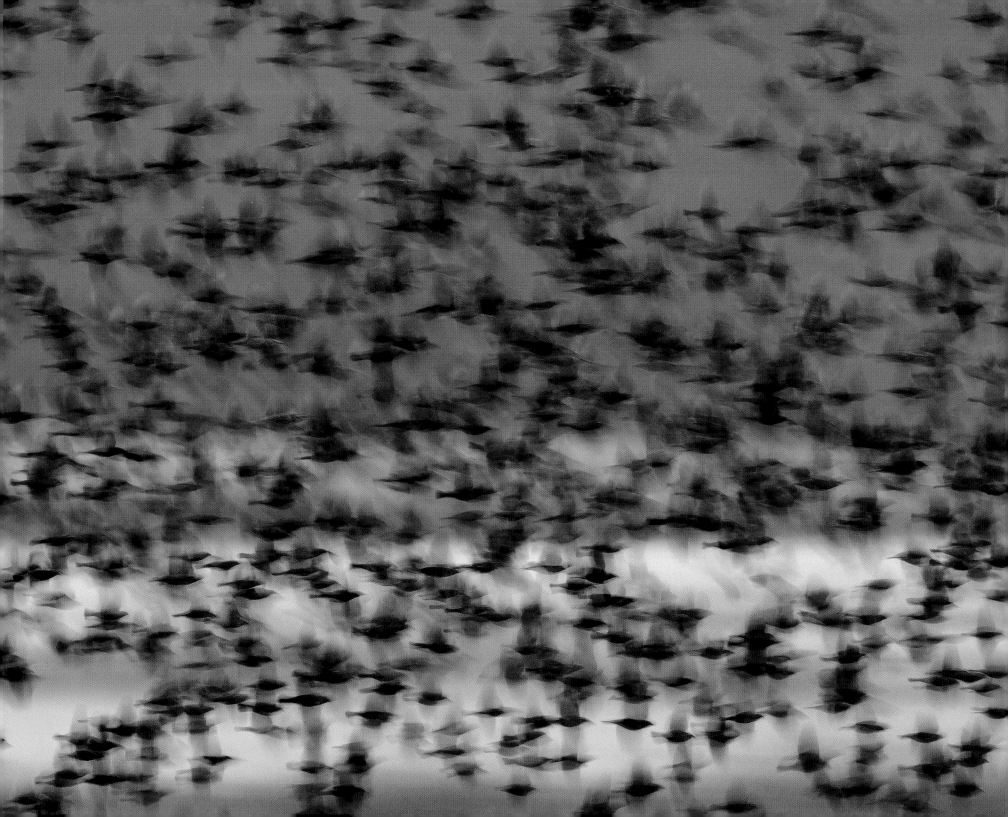

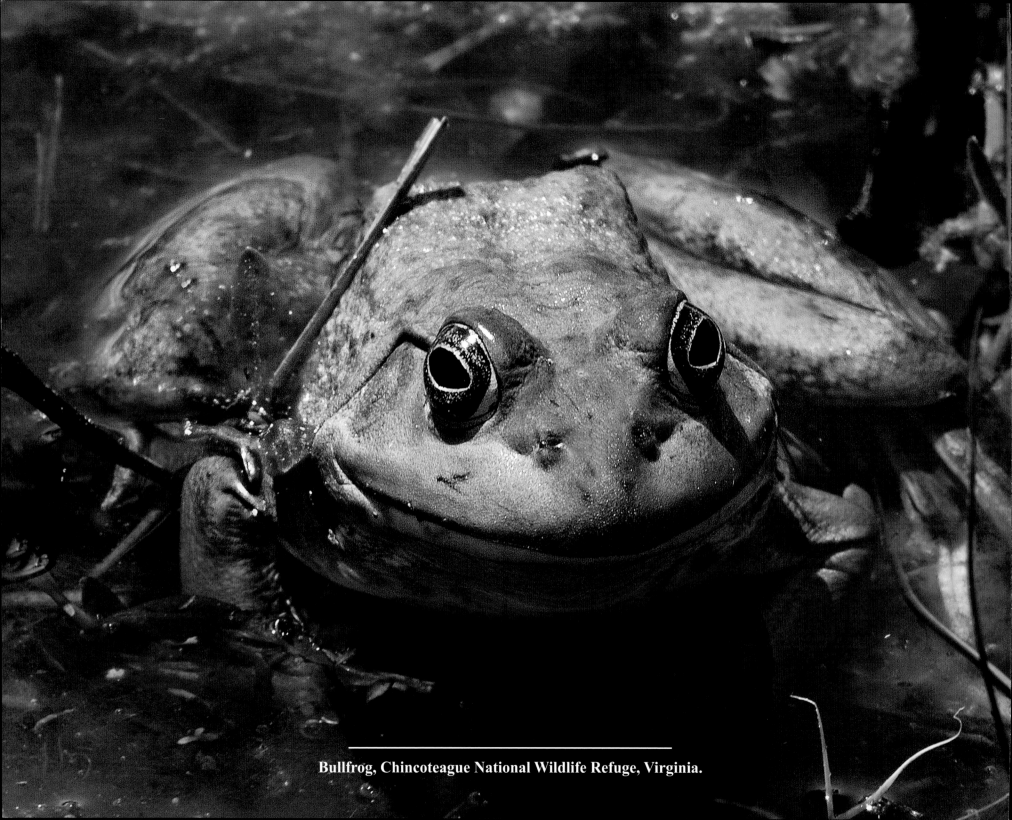

Bullfrog, Chincoteague National Wildlife Refuge, Virginia.

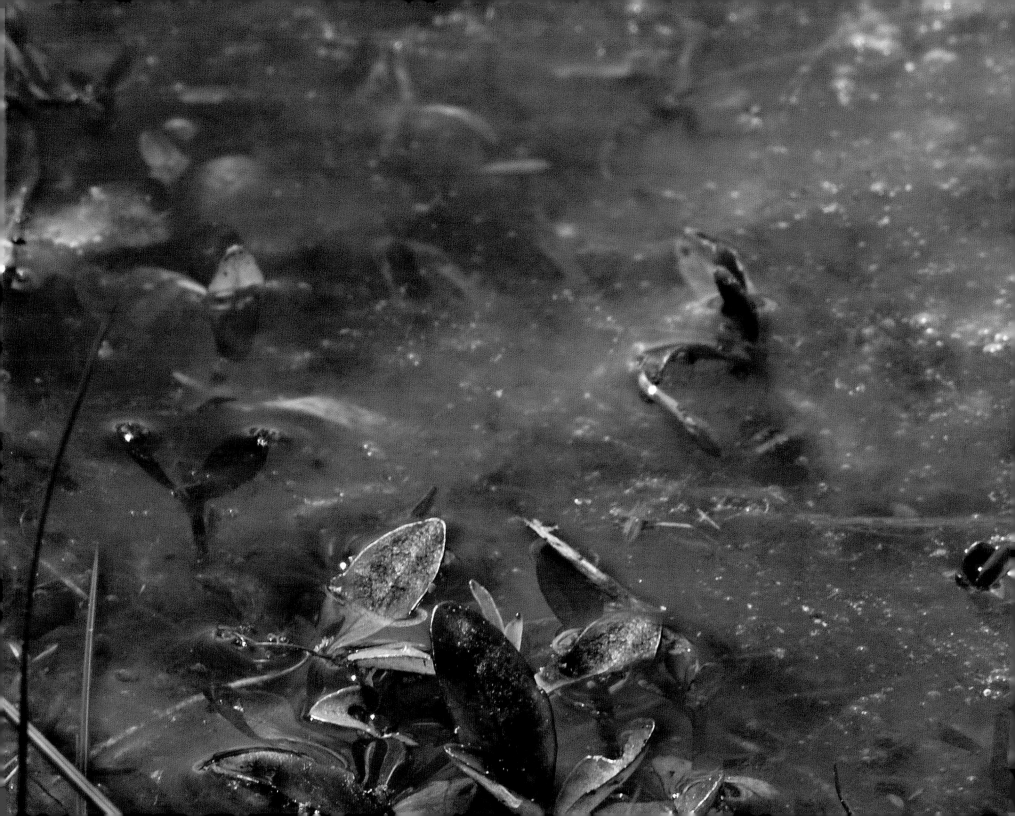

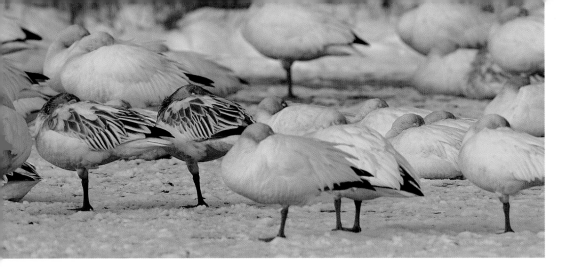

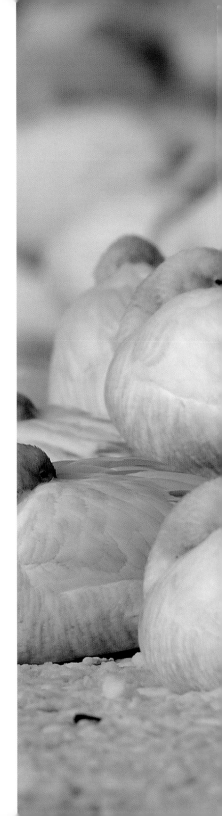

Snow is an uncommon event on Chincoteague. While it does occur along the Eastern Shore, on the island snow isn't something most islanders think about. For them winter means rain, wind, and cold. But when snow happens here, the dunes, marshes, and pine forests become a magical winter wonderland.

In late December 2005, a major east coast snow storm pushed its way across the Eastern Shore, dumping more than ten inches on the island and refuge. Not wanting to pass on the opportunity to photograph this unique situation, I drove the next morning to the island and spent the next two days exploring this wintry coastal landscape. I was amazed and amused to see trucks with snow chains plowing their way along Chincoteague's main road. I was even more amazed to watch a couple of islanders cross-country skiing along Main Street.

The landscape was indeed magical and I roamed the woodlands and marsh trails seeking compositions that would document this rare event. Upon visiting Chincoteague National Wildlife Refuge, I was one of only a handful of hearty explorers taking to this wintry coastal landscape. Near the end of the refuge's Beach Road, snow geese huddled together against the cold wind. Their tawny bellies and black wing feathers stood out in stark contrast to snow-covered ground. I got down on my knees to get a bird's eye view of the snoozing geese. A couple of them kept a watchful gaze on me while the others rested.

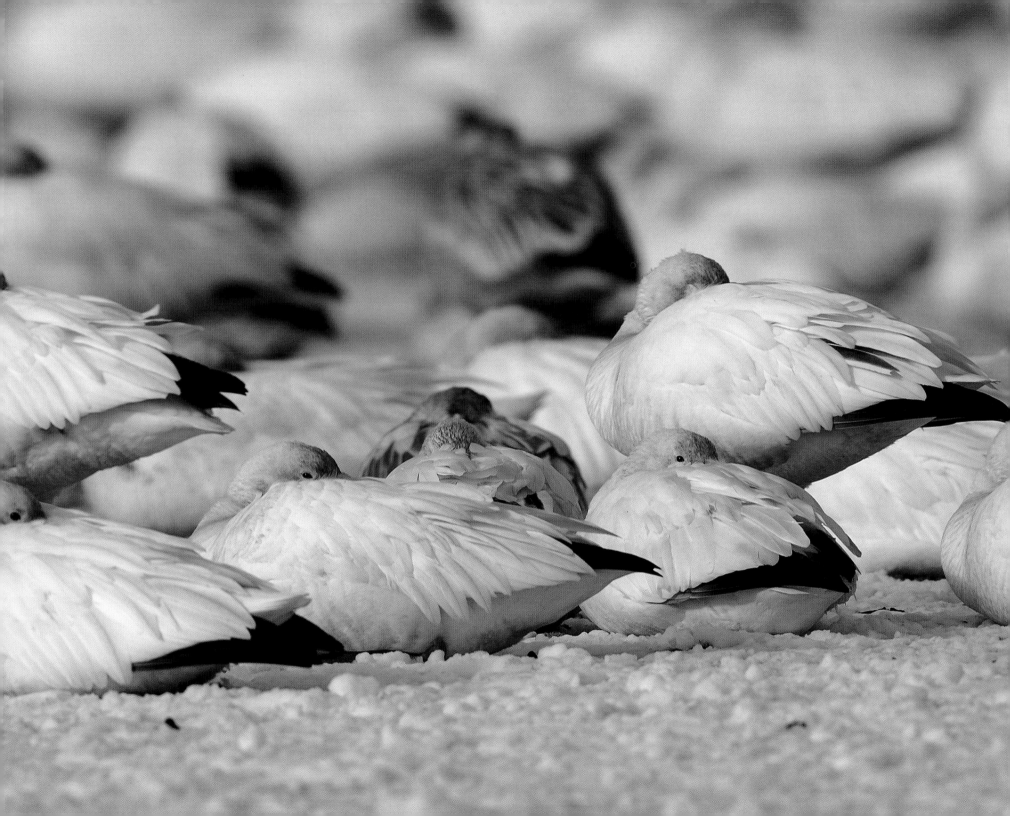

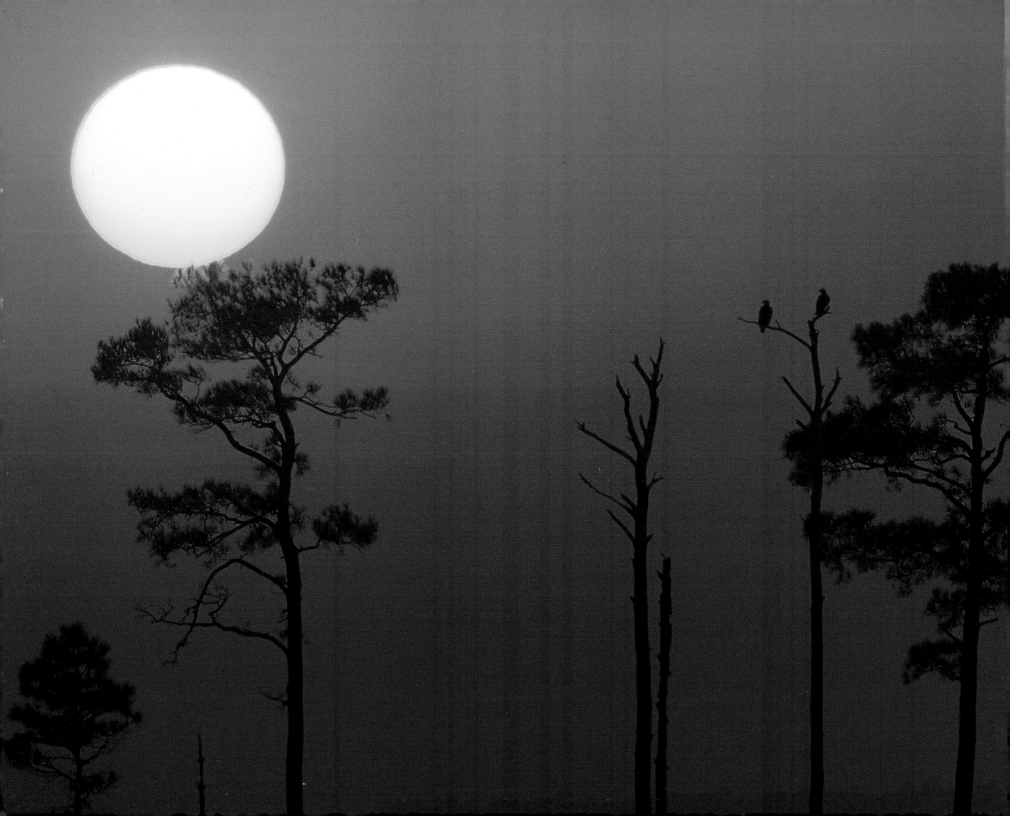

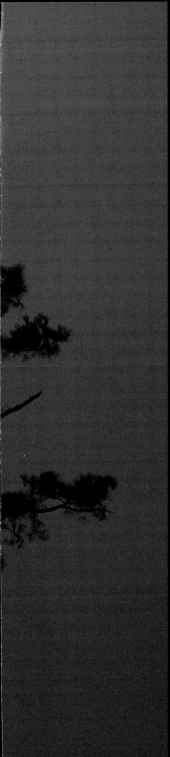

Blackwater National Wildlife Refuge has become the place to see bald eagles in the Mid-Atlantic region. The combination of expansive marshes and scattered loblolly pine snag trees create the right conditions for eagles to feed and nest. There is not a day of the year when one will not see an eagle soaring over the refuge. The refuge and surrounding area have become important wintering areas for the bald eagle. Blackwater also has the highest nesting density of bald eagles in the eastern United States north of Florida.

During one clear spring morning I was driving on the back side of the refuge on Maple Dam Road, which skirts a large expanse of marsh. I stopped at one of my favorite spots along the road to photograph sunrise and I noticed the two bald eagles silhouetted against the ruby-painted sky. As the sun slowly made its way above the horizon, the eagles kept a keen eye on the many flocks of Canada geese rising from the marsh. I used a 600mm telephoto lens to isolate the simple arrangement of loblolly pines in the marsh.

The excitement of capturing this composition was accentuated by all the activity occurring around me that morning. The marsh and woodlands were alive with the songs of song sparrows, mallards, brown-headed nuthatches, geese, flickers, and blue jays. The fresh scent of loblolly pine and marsh grass saturated the spring morning, adding to the sensory overload.

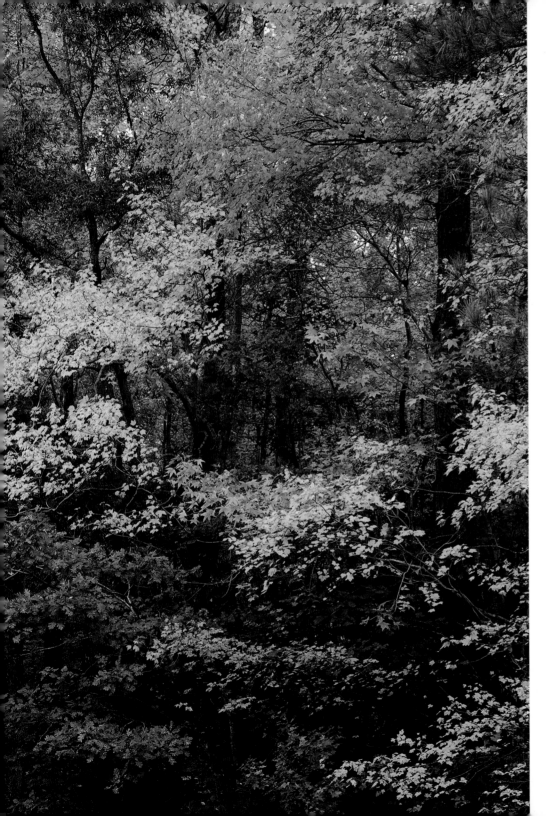

Autumn on the Eastern Shore gives nature photographers and enthusiasts an extra reason to celebrate: infinite possibilities. Here, autumn becomes a gala of colors, critters, landscapes, and memories. Autumn is an energetic season, a season tempting nature photographers with a multitude of photographic subjects. The fall season provides ideal conditions for the nature photographer – fewer crowds, milder temperatures, peak wildlife migrations, and of course, the colorful changing foliage.

Autumn skies here are crispy clear and rich in shades of blue. The migration of millions of birds (and monarch butterflies), from the diminutive songbirds, to graceful raptors, to colorful species of waterfowl and immense flocks of shorebirds, can be seen along the stretches of coastal beach. Add in the rural landscapes and striking coastal vistas, the abstract patterns, and imposing cloud formations dancing across the autumn sky, and you have the makings of a great autumn photography experience.

One November day, while driving along the back roads of Dorchester County, I was surprised by the rich array of fall colors decorating the woodland edges. I was amazed by the saturated hues from the maples, cherries, oaks and sweet gums. This autumn scene was captured at Blackwater National Wildlife Refuge near Cambridge, Maryland.

This image was captured one autumn afternoon at Chincoteague National Wildlife Refuge. My plan was to hike around the auto-tour loop to photograph birds and other wildlife, but when I saw this arrangement of autumn leaves and pine cones nestled on a bed of pine needles, I had to photograph it. With a light overcast sky, the conditions were just right for close-up photography. The overcast skies acted as a giant diffuser, reducing harsh highlights and deep shadows, creating an even tone to the overall composition.

The memory of this moment is a reminder that for me, going from Point A to Point B doesn't always involve a straight line. I'm too curious to make a beeline anywhere these days. It seems that around every corner in nature, I always find something that prevents me from making it in time to my intended destination. That's the magic of nature photography – you never know what will be around the next bend of the trail.

Most nature photographers who visit the Eastern Shore come to photograph the diversity of wildlife that occurs here. But the Eastern Shore's wild heritage is much more than that. It's the diversity of all habitats, life, and processes that makes the region so appealing and for me, addictive.

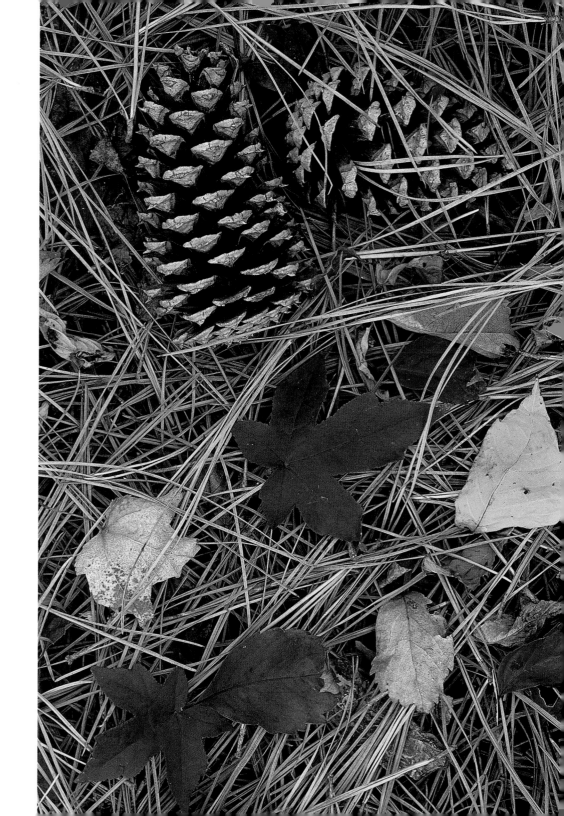

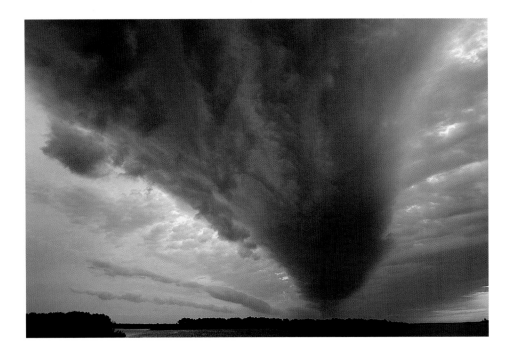

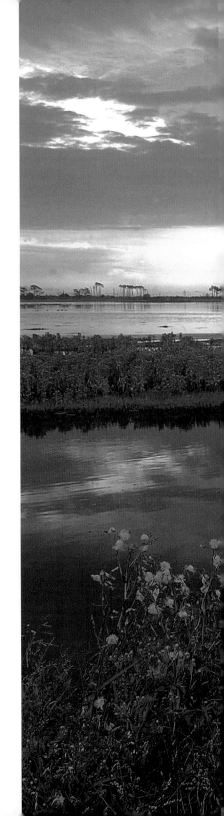

Established in 1943, Chincoteague National Wildlife Refuge is just one of more than 540 national wildlife refuges across the country. To date, every state has at least one national wildlife refuge within its boundaries.

Larger than the National Park Service in terms of the number of units and acreage, the National Wildlife Refuge System's primary purpose is to protect and conserve fish, wildlife, plants, and their habitats. While the National Park Service receives more than 300 million visitors each year to their parks, monuments and historical sites, the National Wildlife Refuge System's annual visitation is about 40 million, and only a handful of national wildlife refuges receive the type of visitation that national parks such as Yellowstone and the Great Smoky Mountains gets.

Because of its close proximity to many major east coast urban centers, Chincoteague's annual visitation exceeds more than 1.4 million. Being next to the Assateague Island National Seashore also adds to the higher visitation rate. However, most of that visitation occurs during the summer months, leaving the fall, winter, and spring to folks who love nature for nature's sake, not just for a sun-tan on the beach.

This image of Snow Goose Pool on the refuge's auto-tour route was captured during a late autumn afternoon.

Above: Winter morning clouds above Chincoteague National Wildlife Refuge, Virginia.

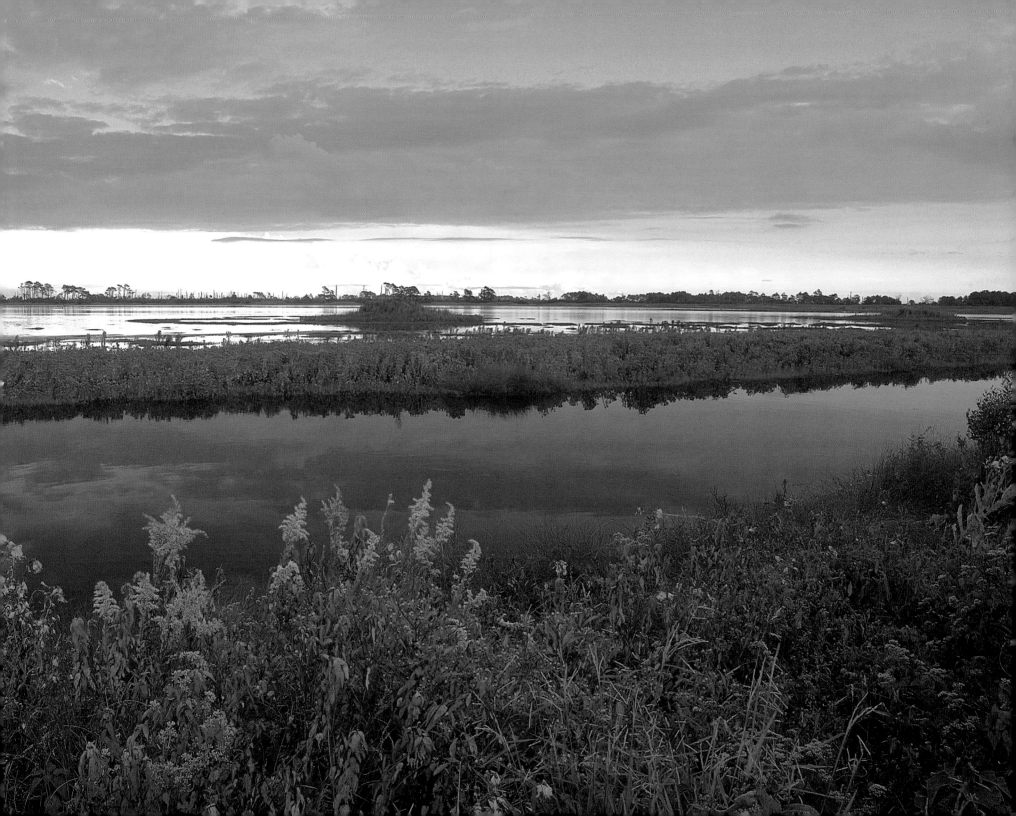

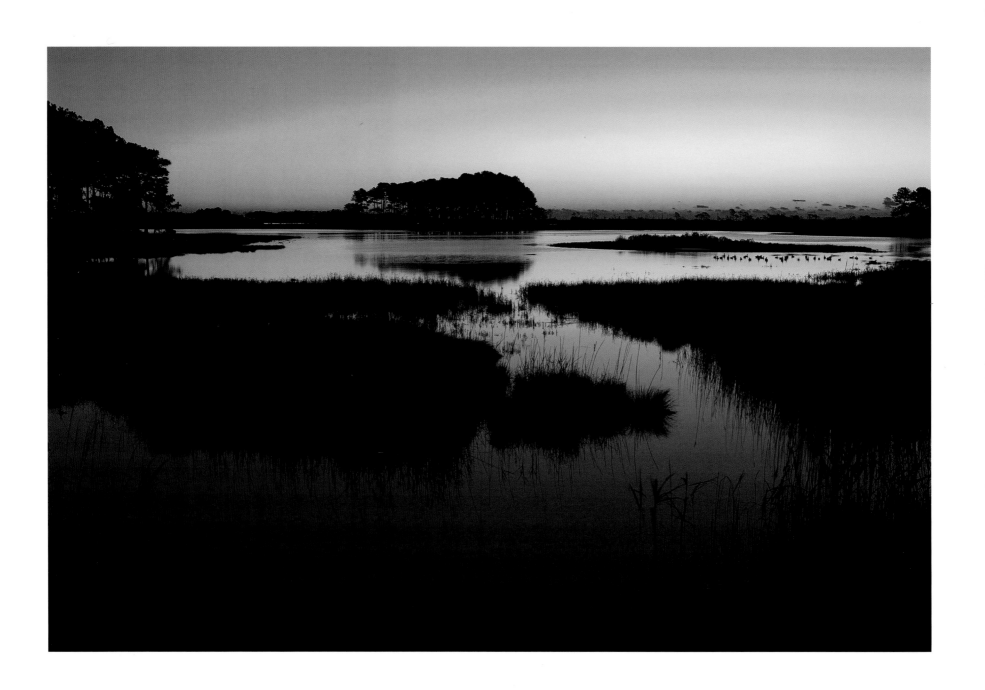

Spring dawn over Black Duck Pool, Chincoteague National Wildlife Refuge, Virginia.